The Wizard of Work

88 Pages to Your Next Job

THE WIZARD OF WORK

88 Pages to Your Next Job

A simple, straightforward job-search book
for people who'd rather be working
than reading a book

RICHARD GAITHER

WITH

JOHN BAKER

Ten Speed Press
Berkeley, California

Ten Speed Press
P.O. Box 7123
Berkeley, CA 94707
www.tenspeed.com

Distributed in Australia by Simon and Schuster Australia, in Canada by Ten Speed Press Canada, in New Zealand by Southern Publishers Group, in South Africa by Real Books, and in the United Kingdom and Europe by Airlift Books.

Cover design by Nancy Austin and Catherine Jacobes

Book design by Victor Ichioka

The author wishes to thank Dr. Albert Lorenzo for permission to use uncopyrighted material. In addition, the following has generously given permission to use quotations from the *Encyclopedia of Prewritten Job Descriptions,* copyright © Business and Legal Reports, Inc.

Library of Congress Cataloging-in-Publication Data

Gaither, Richard.
    The wizard of work / Richard Gaither.
       p. cm.
    Includes bibliographical references.
    ISBN 0-89815-639-4 (pbk.)
     1. Job hunting.   2. Blue collar workers.   3. Employment re-entry.
I. Title.
HF5382.7.G34 1995
650.14—dc20

                            95-6415
                              CIP

Printed in Canada

     14 15 16 17 18 19 20 — 07 06 05 04

Contents

Introduction

The thought behind *88 Pages to Your Next Job* is a simple one! **Most unemployed people tell us that they would rather get their job search rolling than read a book about getting a job**. Because of this, we've eliminated most of the extraneous information that fills the pages of other job search texts and have "cut directly to the chase."

Your objective is to get into the labor market quicker, easier and for higher wages. Ours is to show you one of the best ways to reach that goal. In *88 Pages to Your Next Job*, we're going to draw on 15 years of job search training experience and present only what we think **"you really need to know"** about the most critical job finding competencies...

★ assessing and defining your most marketable skills

★ developing answers to the most problematic interview questions

★ how to persuasively communicate your value to an employer

★ creating simple, but very powerful job search marketing tools

★ planning your job campaign & generating job leads

You won't find stories, jokes, quotes or sections on the world economy and office politics. We're not going to weigh you down with tons of options about resume selection or present you with a myriad of job finding strategies. What you will get is a single direction and a series of proven, power packed exercises and informational pieces that, when read, completed and implemented, will put you head and shoulders above most other job seekers. In other words, we're going to put you through a very systematic process. If you're ready, so is the book and so are we.

Should you have any questions as you go through the activities, please feel free to write or call Dick Gaither, The Wizard of Work at:

Job Search Training Systems, Inc.
7648 Indian Cherry Drive
Nineveh, IN 46164
(800) 361-1613

10 Steps to Finding Your Next Job

Before Anything Else, Know What You Need to Know!

The job search process you're about to enter into is systematically designed to:

★ Counter the most common mistakes made by ill-prepared, uninformed job seekers

★ Answer the questions most frequently asked by frustrated job seekers

The most important and most frequently asked question is: **What are the most important steps to finding my next job?** Our answer to this question previews the 10 steps you'll take to find more satisfying work—in a shorter period of time.

Step 1: Know What You Need to Know

Not understanding what you need to know is usually the first critical mistake by the "hit or miss, hope and pray" job seeker. The hit or miss method, more often than not, leads to extended unemployment and lower yearly salaries.

But knowledge can really power up a job search—and will put you quite a few steps ahead of the average job seeker. Your success will depend to a great degree on what you know about:

★ Yourself and the abilities you can offer to an employer

★ How the labor market operates and screens people

★ The essential functions of the job you are seeking

★ The company, its culture, its products and services, the people in the company, and its hiring practices

Your job search success also relies on your level of commitment: your planning, your willingness to take risks, and your ability to follow up aggressively on any and all leads you generate in your search. To do this well you will need to:

Step 2: Get Yourself into the Right Mind-set

Looking for work by using the more traditional (and less successful) approaches can really wear you down, depress you, and even lead you into taking a position that isn't best for you or your career development. Ask yourself:

Are you willing to use the most successful methods to find the best job for you and to change the way you think about looking for work—even if it means more risk of rejection and more job search activity?

Even though the systematic job search process presented here has high success rates, it can't put you to work without your effort.

Are you willing to commit the needed time, energy, and resources to your search? Chapter 2, "Mind-sets," will help get you in the right frame of mind to do what it takes!

Step 3: Know What You Want

This step has two parts:

1. Define the kind of work you're seeking—what is your realistic and reinforceable job objective? In other words, your objective should be a job you are qualified for (realistic)—and that your experience shows you can do (reinforceable).

One critical error shared by many an unsuccessful job seeker is lack of a vocational focus: a specific and attainable job title. Without a target objective your job search becomes diffused and confused. You need a focus and goals.

Can you name the primary type of work or career you're seeking?

It's always easier to look for a specific job rather than for "anything." It's easier to prepare for one career objective well than to attack a number of career objectives poorly.

Are You Really Ready to Look for Work?

A Quicker Hire and More Money Require You to...

★ Select a realistic job objective

★ Seriously commit to finding work

★ Make social contacts and ask questions

★ Organize and manage your time

★ Realistically analyze your skills and value

★ Develop powerful interviewing skills

★ Create screen-proof job search tools

★ Take calculated risks and be creative

2. Determine what you want in return for your labor and loyalty.

Everyone works for different reasons. Do you know what rings your bells?

- ★ Determine the lowest dollar you're willing to take
- ★ Determine your smallest acceptable benefits package
- ★ Identify 10 job satisfaction factors that you want from your next job

Now you're ready to move on to:

Step 4: Determine What You Can Offer an Employer (Skills Analysis)

The most successful job seekers know what they have to offer an employer and can usually offer more than their competition.

- ★ Identify your most marketable (and reinforceable) job-specific skills, transferable skills, and fitting-in skills (personality traits)
- ★ Identify your most powerful and relevant life, work, and educational achievements
- ★ Learn to analyze a job title and description for critical skills
- ★ Use job descriptions and government publications to build a "screen-proof" career vocabulary
- ★ Create a job opportunity generator

Step 5: Do Company Research to Match Your Skills to the Employers' Needs

If you don't know the rules of the game of the field and company you want to be part of, I can guarantee you won't make it past the first cut. Research, first into the field and then into the companies of your choice, will give you a working edge over your competition and drastically reduce the number of times you get screened out.

- ★ Determine general hiring practices within the field
- ★ Find out about each company's culture, services and products, and personnel
- ★ Learn how employers use gatekeepers to screen people in—but mostly out of—the interview

Step 6: Create Competition-Beating, Easy-to-Build Job Search Tools

Every job seeker needs the right tools for the job, but most people just won't take the time to create them. Solid job search tools build your confidence, get you into the door more often, and keep you in the mind's eye of the employer for longer periods.

- ★ Develop screen-proof **resumes**
- ★ Power-up your **application** process
- ★ Design attention-grabbing **cover letters**
- ★ Create memorable follow-up and **thank-you notes**
- ★ Build an unforgettable promotional **career card**

Step 7: Learn to Handle Interviews with Skill; Know What Employers Want to Hear

The interview is where the decision is made. Chapter 7 will teach you how to do it right!

- ★ Learn how each employer makes hiring decisions
- ★ Reduce your interview fear and build your confidence
- ★ Learn to open and close the interview with power
- ★ Persuasively communicate your value to employers
- ★ Develop answers to the most problematic questions
- ★ Learn what questions to ask the interviewer
- ★ Exhibit traits that get you on a second-interview list
- ★ Use post-interview follow-up procedures

Step 8: Generate Job Leads and Interviews

- ★ Create a personal referral network
- ★ Learn phone lead techniques that . . .
  - generate 30 leads per day
  - get you past the secretarial blockade
  - counter employer's objections
- ★ Expand the list of companies who use your skills
- ★ Respond to help-wanted ads more effectively
- ★ Use resume databases to expand your opportunity

Step 9: Manage Your Job Search Time and Keep Your Sanity!

The unsuccessful job seeker is often hurt by lack of organization and time management skills. Chapter 9 will show you how to build these skills in no time to power up your search.

★ Use only the most successful job search strategies

★ Develop job search support systems

★ Structure your day and track your activities

★ Enter group job search classes for quicker success

Step 10: Choose Your Best Offer

Know how to get the best job—on the best terms! In Chapter 10 we'll help you make the best decision.

Mind-sets
How to Get the Attitude that Gets a Job

Job seekers often create their own negative reality by the behaviors they exhibit. They actually *sabotage* their job search! To counter this problem, you need to develop the correct mind-set—remember, if the head's not working, neither will the body.

Here are a few mind-set issues to consider:

1. **Taking Control** Job search magic requires that you be willing to choose a career and move toward it, accepting responsibility for your own career life.

2. **Rejection** Don't flush your life down the toilet just because of a little rejection. There *is* life after rejection. Other people have had to deal with setbacks— and lived through it. Figure on going to 20– 40 interviews before you find the job you really want.

Formula for Job Search Failure

Negative self-talk = negative self-image = negative impression = extended unemployment

3. **Being Assertive** Interviews have only one winner. Those who hold their own ground during the interview usually win the prize. Be assertive, but do it with style!

4. **"Self Talk"** Talk yourself into success. Every time you meet a prospective employer, describe yourself and your career history in positive terms. Don't dwell on your shortcomings or failures— you're looking for work you *can* do, not work you can't. If you don't think you can do the job well, you can count on the interviewer getting the same message. On the other hand, people who think they'll get the job usually do!

5. **Playing Your Hunches** There may be a lot of truth to the statement, "If it feels right, do it!" It's nothing to count on, but sometimes dumb luck succeeds where careful planning and attention to detail have not. Keep your mind open and work on every possiblity that crosses your path.

6. **Faking It** Fake it—until you can make it. Exhibit the traits most commonly associated with "peak performers." Sooner or later they'll become a part of you.

7. **Smiling** Employers like to see a smile. People who smile usually get more consideration. Besides, smiling makes you feel good.

8. **Half Full** When the going gets tough, always think of your glass as being half full, not half empty. If you think in a half empty fashion, you'll run out of job search juice too quickly to generate success.

Peak Performer Traits

Calmness under Pressure
High Energy Level
Steady Focus
Expectation of Positive Outcomes

9. **Commitment** Don't delay and don't waste time on nonproductive activities. Do the exercises, take the risks, use the techniques, and invest the time to do things right—the first time.

10. **Health** Take care of yourself, get physical, exercise! Don't victimize yourself with job search stress.

11. **Talking** Talk with successful people. Don't be intimidated by them. Powerful people like to tell their story, answer well-thought-out questions, and help other people emulate their success.

12. **Taking Risks** Be ready to step in over your head at times. There's a direct relationship between the risk you take, the quality of the job you acquire, and the speed with which you acquire it.

13. **Learning** Be willing to learn from your mistakes and from the experiences of others. Keep yourself from behind the unemployment eight ball.

3 Job Objectives

How to Define a Realistic and Reinforceable Job Objective and Determine What You Want from Your Next Job

If you don't target a realistic and reinforceable job objective—a job you are qualified for, and that your experience shows you can do—you won't avoid one of the most destructive of all job search mistakes: looking for an "I'll do anything" job.

Why Is This So Important?

★ Most employers identify the lack of a career focus as a main reason for applicant rejection.

★ You have to know what type of work you want in order to create a powerful career vocabulary that relates your past experience to the job demands.

★ You keep your sanity and generate quicker success by focusing your presentation and paperwork on one specific job search area rather than on many different ones.

How Do You Know If You Have a Realistic and Reinforceable Job Objective?

If the work you're looking for meets these three criteria...

1. You really want to do it!
2. You can do it very well, right now!
3. You know why you like this type of work!

and if your answer to these four questions is yes . . .

1. Do your skills match the job demands?
2. Does your education meet the job demands?
3. Do your abilities meet the job demands?
4. Does your experience meet the job demands?

then you have a realistic and reinforceable job objective!

If you don't know what you're looking for, it's really hard to find it!

Lessons from Life

Follow Your Own Star and Develop Career Success

The following are some of the lessons I have learned from personal experience and observation over the past twenty-five years of business and professional life. They are offered for consideration by those who seek to accelerate the learning process by profiting from someone else's experience, rather than just their own.

• There is no substitute for effort.

• Never assume—act only on what you know to be true.

• Truth is the strongest argument.

• Success has two requirements: doing the right things and doing things right.

• The pendulum always swings equally in both directions.

• When you stop learning, you stop living.

• People judge what they can't see by what they can see.

• The first one to get angry usually loses.

• Listen at least twice as much as you talk.

• Give your word cautiously, and keep your word faithfully.

• Saving time begins by taking time.

• The only thing worse than lying to others is lying to yourself.

• If you've never failed, you've probably never really tried.

• We always walk the fastest when we're lost.

Dr. Albert J. Lorenzo
President, Macomb Community College, Warren, Michigan

What Do You Do If You Can't Name the Type of Work You Want?

Cheat! It's fair in a job search. Appendix A (page 77) has a big list of job titles, gathered from a number of job description books. Read it over, and select the title that best matches the type of work you want.

• What If You Still Can't Define a Job Objective?

Get *The Quick Job-Hunting Map* by Dick Bolles (Berkeley, CA: Ten Speed Press, 1990), or contact your local Job Training Partnership Act (see page 86) or job service office, talk with a certified career counselor, or give us a call at (800) 361-1613. We might be able to help you!

Job Satisfaction Factors

A perfect job is where you're overpaid to underwork! You've got to recognize that there aren't many of these perfect jobs left! Even so, you can greatly enhance your job satisfaction if you know how important each of the following factors are to you. The question is: What do you want in return for the use of your labor, time, skills, and knowledge.

• Let's Talk Money First!

Without a well-thought-out expense budget, you won't be able to determine if you can take a job at the stated salary or if you should negotiate for higher pay.

Rent/mortgage	$	Work parking	$
Home insurance	$	Work transport	$
Home maintenance	$	Work meals	$
State taxes	$	Child care	$
Federal taxes	$	Clothing	$
Car payment	$	Education	$
License plates	$	Entertainment	$
Car insurance	$	Hobbies	$
Car gas/oil	$	Memberships	$
Car maintenance	$	Subscriptions	$
Life insurance	$	Credit cards	$
Disability insurance	$	Sewer fee	$
Health insurance	$	Trash pick-up	$
Water	$	Cable TV	$
Heat	$		$
Electricity	$		$

THIS IS THE LOWEST BUCK I CAN TAKE $ _____

• Define Your Job Satisfaction Factors

Too many people in today's labor market are on a career treadmill. They're going no place, fast and without a smile. They never give any real thought to what rings their bell—aside from a paycheck—and become dissatisfied, stagnated workers.

Job Satisfaction and Self-Motivation Factors

Will the job satisfy your inner self?

Will you really get to do what you want to do?

What's most important to you?

Top 15 Factors Identified as Very Important When Accepting a Job*—Money is #16!

65% want open communication

60% want less job/family interference

59% want quality management

59% want realistic work duties

58% want supervisory competence

55% want control over work content

55% want to gain new skills

54% want job security

53% want quality coworkers

50% want good location

50% want stimulating work

46% want family support policies

43% want good fringe benefits

38% want to control work schedule

37% want advancement opportunity

* From the National Study of the Changing Workforce, Families and Work Institute, 1993.

4 Skills Identification
How to Identify Your Most Marketable Skills

What is a skill? Any special knowledge, behavior, trait, or capability for which an employer will pay you!

The World of Skills

• Is There More Than One Type of Skill?

You betcha! Employers know that the best employees can bring three distinct sets of skills to the job. You use these skills during the job search, too.

Can You Do the Job? (Job Skills) The good applicant understands the daily demands, duties, and responsibilities of the job. Can you "walk the walk" as well as "talk the talk"? Can you operate the tools of your chosen field?

Job skills are usually outlined in a job description and provide the baseline for the employer's initial evaluation of you as a worker.

To insure that you don't screen yourself out, you'll need to develop a "career vocabulary" for the field you wish to enter. These are the words used to describe your job's primary daily duties and responsibilities, and they tend to be unique to a specific occupation. These words will demonstrate that you have the basic skills, abilities, experience, and special knowledge to be considered for the initial, "screening" interview. Without this vocabulary you are dead meat.

Will You Get Along? (Fitting-in Skills) Does your personality fit the field, the company, the co-workers, and the supervisors? Nothing destroys a working environment faster than someone who dislikes his or her job and refuses to get along.

Even though employers are increasingly using personality profile tests, honesty tests, and drug tests to determine if you're the kind of person they want on the payroll, most employers still do this sort of assessment during the interview.

The easiest way to make sure your personality matches the job you're seeking is to complete our personality traits checklist (see pages 9–10) and question the people who do the hiring in your line of work.

Do You Have Other Skills? (Transferable Skills) Can you identify other life, work, or educational experiences that can readily *transfer* to the job you're now seeking? The more transferable skills you have, the easier it is to convince an employer that you will generate added value for the company.

These skills are usually discussed during the first and second interviews. They allow the employer to make an even more detailed comparison of all the applicants' capabilities. By doing a good job of identifying this set of skills, you'll be able to negotiate for more money and a better benefit package.

Even though it will take a little bit of time to identify your transferable skills, it's well worth the effort. The easiest way to gather this information is by selecting your skills from the extensive transferable skills list on pages 11–16.

• Which Kind of Skill Is the Most Important in the Job Search?

They're all equally important—they're just "most important" at different times:

> **Job skills** are most important in developing screen-proof job search tools.
>
> **Fitting-in skills** are most important when making your first impression.
>
> **Transferable skills** sway things your way at interviews.

Identifying Your Most Marketable and Reinforceable Skills

The problem with trying to identify your skills isn't that you don't have them. *All God's children got skills!*

Most job seekers don't realize that these three sets of skills are sought by employers. Other people just can't find the right words to describe the skills they know they have. We'll help you find out what job, fitting-in, and transferable skills you have, so you can communicate them to employers!

The Job Seeker's World Revolves Around Skills Identification

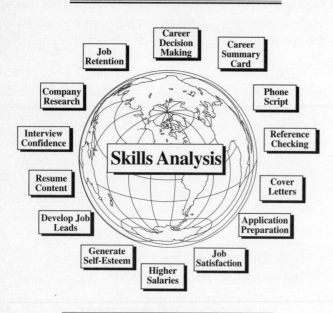

Job Retention · Career Decision Making · Career Summary Card · Company Research · Phone Script · Interview Confidence · Reference Checking · Resume Content · Cover Letters · Develop Job Leads · Application Preparation · Generate Self-Esteem · Job Satisfaction · Higher Salaries

Skills Analysis

Skills Identification
Your First...And Most Important...Activity!

• Identify Your Job Skills

Every facet of career selection, career development, and job search success revolves around your ability to identify, analyze, and prioritize your skills. Yet fewer than 2 job seekers in 10 can actually answer the most important question you will ever ask of yourself and which every interviewer will ask of you: **What are your most marketable and reinforceable skills?** In other words, why should the employer hire you? What do you have that an employer wants? What special skills and abilities do you possess that an employer would pay good money to use?

Ask Yourself That Question.

Give it a shot! In five minutes, try to write down every job skill you think you can bring to your next employer.

1. _____
2. _____
3. _____
4. _____
5. _____
6. _____
7. _____
8. _____
9. _____
10. _____
11. _____
12. _____
13. _____
14. _____
15. _____
16. _____
17. _____
18. _____
19. _____
20. _____
21. _____
22. _____
23. _____
24. _____
25. _____
26. _____
27. _____
28. _____
29. _____
30. _____

If you really want to get that job offer, you've got to know yourself and what job skills you can offer an employer that are better than the skills of others who are competing for the job!

Does your vocabulary tell the employer that you'll fit in with company policies, daily job functions, your co-workers and supervisors?

That'll be you right there.

• Fitting-in Skills

If you've ever worked with someone who's a real pain in the butt, you'll understand why one of America's biggest employee problems is people who don't fit in with the team. Clearly, you don't want to be one of them. And you want to convince any prospective employer that you won't be a problem. So here's a way to identify those personality traits that make you an outstanding team player.

• Identify Your Fitting-in Skills

★ **First step:** In the Personality Trait Checklist on pages 9–10, circle each word you think really describes your personality.

★ **Second step:** Review the words you've circled. Ask yourself, "Is this a personality trait an employer would consider a positive one—for the job I want?"

★ **Third step:** From your second-step list, choose your top 20 traits.

1. _____
2. _____
3. _____
4. _____
5. _____
6. _____
7. _____
8. _____
9. _____
10. _____
11. _____
12. _____
13. _____
14. _____
15. _____
16. _____
17. _____
18. _____
19. _____
20. _____

Enter these traits into your job offer generator grid (page 21). Now you have the words to convince employers you won't be a pain at work.

Personality Trait Checklist

Academic	Candid	Courageous
Accurate	Capable	Creative
Active	Careful	Critical
Adaptable	Caring	Curious
Adept	Cautious	Daring
Adventurous	Challenges, likes	Deliberate
Affectionate		Democratic
Aggressive	Charming	Dependable
Alert	Cheerful	Detailed
Ambitious	Clear-thinking	Determined
Analytical	Clever	Dignified
Arrogant	Competent	Diplomatic
Artistic	Competitive	Disciplined
Assertive	Composed	Discreet
Astute	Concerned	Discriminating
Attentive	Confident	Dominating
Attractive	Conforming	Dynamic
Authentic	Conscientious	Eager
Authoritative	Conservative	Easygoing
Aware	Considerate	Eccentric
Bold	Consistent	Economical
Brash	Constructive	Effective
Broadminded	Conventional	Efficient
Businesslike	Cool	Empathic
Calm	Cooperative	Energetic

Enterprising

Enthusiastic

Exceptional

Exhibitionistic

Experienced

Expert

Expressive

Extravagant

Fair-minded

Far-sighted

Firm

Flexible

Flirtatious

Forceful

Forgiving

Formal

Frank

Friendly

Generous

Gentle

Good character

Good-natured

Gracious

Healthy

Helpful

Honest

Humanistic

Humorous

Idealistic

Imaginative

Impulsive

Independent

Individualistic

Industrious

Informal

Ingenious

Innovative

Insightful

Inspiring

Integrity, has

Intellectual

Intuitive

Inventive

Kind

Leisurely

Light-hearted

Likable

Logical

Loyal

Materialistic

Mature

Methodical

Meticulous

Mild-mannered

Moderate

Modest

Natural

Neat

Nonconforming

Objective

Obliging

Open-minded

Opportunistic

Optimistic

Orderly

Organized

Original

Outgoing

Outstanding

Painstaking

Patient

Peaceable

Penetrating

Perceptive

Perfectionistic

Persevering

Persistent

Philosophical

Pioneering

Playful

Pleasant

Pleasure-
seeking

Poised

Polite

Positive

Practical

Precise

Productive

Progressive

Proud

Prudent

Punctual

Purposeful

Quick

Quick thinking

Quiet

Rational

Realistic

Reasonable

Reflective

Relaxed

Reliable

Reserved

Resourceful

Respectful

Responsible

Retiring

Risk-taking

Robust

Self-confident

Self-controlled

Self-reliant

Sense of humor

Sensible

Sensitive

Sentimental

Serious

Sharp-witted

Shrewd

Sincere

Sociable

Sophisticated

Spontaneous

Spunky

Stable

Steady

Strong-willed

Successful

Sympathetic

Tactful

Talkative

Teachable

Tenacious

Thorough

Thoughtful

Thrifty

Tidy

Tolerant

Tough

Trusting

Trustworthy

Unassuming

Uncommon

Understanding

Unexcitable

Uninhibited

Unique

Verbal

Versatile

Vigorous

Visionary

Warm

Witty

• Transferable Skills

Transferable skills are the hottest new item on every interviewer's wish list. These are the skills that you bring from other life, work, and educational experiences. The more of them that you have and can talk about during the interview, the more value you create for yourself.

• Why Is Naming These Skills So Valuable?

It shows the interviewer that you can give the company more than just the basic performance of the job for which you're applying. A good supply of transferable skills will help convince the employer that you're a better dollar value than the competition. Not only that—you show the employer that you've given considerable thought to what you have to offer. (Be sure you can back up everything you say during the interview.)

• Identify Your Transferable Skills

This is one of the most comprehensive skills listings to be found anywhere. But we want to make you stand apart from the competition—and by doing a thorough job of identifying your transferable skills, you can!

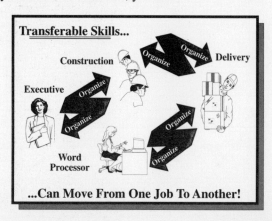

Career Failure Formula

Don't take the time + Don't invest the effort = Your future

★ **Step 1** Put a check mark ✓ next to each transferable skill you use on a regular basis—but only if you can give three or more examples of when you've successfully used the skill. (If you can't come up with the examples, don't even think about checking it.)

★ **Step 2** Review each check-marked ✓ skill and double-check ✓ ✓ if it's a skill that will probably be regularly used in the job being sought.

Transferable Skills: What Are You Really Good at Doing?

1. Abstract or conceptualize ideas
2. Act as liaison, go-between, or intermediary
3. Act or perform for audiences
4. Adapt to changing situations and needs
5. Adapt tools, machinery, and equipment
6. Address or talk to individual people and groups
7. Adjust, arrange, or adapt information
8. Adjust or align tools or equipment
9. Administer projects or events
10. Advise people
11. Aim or shoot straight
12. Allocate, disperse, or give away resources
13. Amuse people
14. Analyze information, data, or situations
15. Analyze tasks
16. Anticipate problems and unusual situations
17. Apply finishes, like paints or protectants
18. Apply information from one situation to another
19. Appraise or evaluate work or services
20. Approve or "OK" the behavior of others
21. Approve or "OK" expenditures
22. Arbitrate or solve problems between people
23. Arrange or organize social gatherings
24. Arrange or organize tools or equipment
25. Assemble or collect data or information
26. Assemble or collect materials
27. Assemble or get people together
28. Assess a person's performance
29. Assess or analyze data or information
30. Assess or analyze people
31. Assess situations
32. Assess the performance of equipment
33. Assign/delegate duties and/or responsibilities
34. Attend or pay attention to detail
35. Attract attention to yourself, others, or ideas
36. Audit or balance financial information
37. Balance objects acrobatically
38. Balance schedules, duties, and tasks
39. Bargain or barter
40. Be innovative, come up with new ideas
41. Bind or wrap items
42. Blast things apart
43. Breed animals
44. Budget money
45. Budget time or resources
46. Build things with tools and equipment
47. Build trust and confidence
48. Calculate or compute numbers
49. Carpet floors
50. Carry, lift, and load
51. Carry out either your own or others' plans
52. Catch objects
53. Chair or oversee meetings
54. Chart or graph information
55. Check information for accuracy
56. Check materials or products for quality/quantity
57. Classify information, data, or objects
58. Clean or clear
59. Clerical work
60. Climb
61. Climb a mountain
62. Coach
63. Collaborate or work with others on a project
64. Collate or sort data
65. Collate or sort objects, materials, or papers
66. Collect information
67. Collect money
68. Committee work

69. Communicate data or information
70. Communicate warmth and care
71. Compare information, data
72. Compare objects
73. Compile or collect information
74. Complete projects or tasks on schedule
75. Compose articles, reports, or other documents
76. Compose music
77. Confer or talk with others to make decisions
78. Confront others
79. Construct buildings
80. Construct tools, machines, or equipment
81. Consult with others
72. Contract with others
83. Control costs
84. Control crisis situations
85. Control situations, people, events, etc.
86. Control tools, machines, or equipment
87. Converse or talk with others
88. Convey feelings or emotions
89. Cook
90. Cooperate with others
91. Cope with deadlines and time pressure
92. Cope with difficulties, solve problems
93. Copy information, data, or drawings
94. Correct mistakes
95. Correspond with others
96. Count, inventory, keep track
97. Create things from your own ideas
98. Critique or review others' work
99. Critique or review products and services
100. Cultivate crops and plants
102. Cut to measurement
102. Dance
103. Deal with people
104. Deal with unknowns
105. Debate or argue a point
106. Decorate
107. Define how things are to be done
108. Delegate work
109. Deliver things
110. Deliver work as promised
111. Demonstrate fashion
112. Demonstrate how to do things

113. Design for beauty
114. Detail out projects
115. Detect problems or errors
116. Develop ideas or prototypes
117. Develop rapport
118. Diagnose problems
119. Direct people or projects
120. Discipline others
121. Discriminate colors
122. Dispatch or route information or materials
123. Dispense medicines
124. Display things
125. Dissect animals, insects, etc.
126. Distribute items, products
127. Divert attention from one thing to another
128. Draft or draw inanimate objects
129. Dramatize situations
130. Draw charts, pictures, or graphics
131. Draw samples from animals, plants, earth
132. Drill holes in things
133. Drill wells
134. Drive machines or vehicles
135. Edit film or videotape
136. Edit written material
137. Empathize with people's situations
138. Empower others
139. Encourage others
140. Endure long hours
141. Endure personal hardships
142. Enforce rules and regulations
143. Enlarge things
144. Enlighten others
145. Enlist others to help complete a job
146. Entertain people
147. Establish policy or procedures
148. Estimate cost, distance, size, etc.
149. Evaluate yourself or others
150. Examine for detail
151. Execute, implement, get something done
152. Exercise diplomacy
153. Exercise discretion
154. Exhibit or demonstrate products, ideas
155. Exhibit good finger dexterity
156. Expand

157. Expedite, speed up
158. Experiment
159. Explain
160. Explore
161. Express attitudes
162. Express feelings
163. Express thoughts
164. Fabricate
165. Facilitate
166. Farm
167. Feed animals, plants, or people
168. File records or information
169. Fill orders or requests
170. Financial planning
171. Find things or information
172. Fit things together
173. Fix or repair
174. Follow directions
175. Follow through on tasks
176. Forecast what will happen
177. Forge metals
178. Formulate ideas
179. Garden
180. Gather data or information
181. Gather objects or materials
182. Govern
183. Graphically illustrate
184. Grind
185. Groundskeeping
186. Group people
187. Group things
188. Group work
189. Grow plants, flowers, crops
190. Guide
191. Hand-crafted work
192. Handle complaints
193. Handle dangerous equipment or materials
194. Handle emergencies
195. Handle multiple tasks simultaneously
196. Handle or move things
197. Handle sophisticated equipment
198. Harmonize
199. Help animals
200. Help people
201. Hike, camp out, and survive in wilderness
202. Hire and fire people
203. Hit objects
204. Host events
205. Identify and seize on opportunities
206. Identify problems
207. Identify resources
208. Identify similarities
209. Illustrate or depict
210. Imagine
211. Impersonate others
212. Implement decisions, plans, or ideas
213. Impress people
214. Improve situations
215. Improve systems or procedures
216. Improve tools, machines, or equipment
217. Improvise
218. Index or organize data or information
219. Influence, persuade, or convince others
220. Inform or give out information to others
221. Inquire or do research
222. Inspect for quality
223. Inspire others to do better
224. Install or service equipment
225. Instruct or train people
226. Integrate data or information
227. Interpret body language
228. Interpret data, information, or charts
229. Interpret foreign language
230. Interpret symbols on drawings or charts
231. Interview people for information
232. Invent
233. Investigate
234. Isolate causes, elements, or items
235. Judge truth or accuracy
236. Justify attitudes, decisions, or conclusions
237. Keep books
238. Keep secrets or confidential information
239. Keep or track details or information
240. Knead
241. Knit
242. Lab work
243. Landscape

244. Lay tile or linoleum flooring
245. Lead others
246. Learn quickly
247. Lift heavy, medium, or light weights
248. Listen perceptively
249. Load or unload materials
250. Locate information, things, or data
251. Locate people
252. Maintain tolerances, standards, or limits
253. Make contacts
254. Make decisions
255. Make layouts
256. Make models
257. Make or set policy
258. Make referrals to others
259. Make recommendations, give advice
260. Manage money
261. Manage time
262. Manipulate data
263. Manipulate ideas
264. Manipulate people
265. Manual dexterity, eye-hand coordination
266. Map out land, water, or air areas
267. Market research
268. Mathematics
269. Measure boundaries, sizes, or weights
270. Mechanical reasoning
271. Mediate disputes or problems
272. Meet and greet the public
273. Memorize large amounts of information
274. Mentor others
275. Merge or combine ideas or systems
276. Mobilize resources and people
277. Model clothing or accessories
278. Moderate situations
279. Modify, mold, or change behavior
280. Mold things into shape
281. Monitor machines, equipment, processes
282. Motivate others to do better work
283. Move quickly
284. Navigate
285. Negotiate
286. Not show emotions
287. Nurture human growth

288. Nurture plants or animals
289. Observe and monitor data, people, or things
290. Obtain information
291. Operate an independent business
292. Operate tools, machinery, or equipment
293. Operate vehicles
294. Oral presentations
295. Order supplies
296. Organize data or information
297. Organize ideas
298. Organize people
299. Organize tools, machines, equipment, things
300. Originate new ideas or procedures
301. Paint houses—interiors or exteriors
302. Paint pictures
303. Perceive needs of others
304. Persuade or convince people
305. Photography
306. Plan projects or tasks
307. Plant crops or flowers
308. Plant ideas
309. Play games
310. Play a musical instrument
311. Play politics
312. Precision work
313. Predict outcomes
314. Prepare or make things ready
315. Present information, products, ideas
316. Preserve antiques
317. Preserve ideas or beliefs
318. Preside over meetings
319. Press an issue
320. Press clothing
321. Print by hand
322. Process information, data, or people
323. Produce or direct
324. Program computers
325. Project future events
326. Project vocally
327. Promote ideas, products, or people
328. Proofread
329. Protect people or property
330. Punch or box
331. Purchase or buy

332. Put in order: systems or processes
333. Put in order: tools, machines, or objects
334. Question or query
335. Raise funds
336. Ranch work
337. Reach or achieve goals
338. Read and use reference materials
339. Recognize obsolescence
340. Reconcile financial records
341. Reconcile personal differences
342. Record or log data, information
343. Recreate, duplicate, or reproduce products
344. Recreate situations or experiments
345. Recruit people
346. Reduce budgets or services
347. Reduce or make things smaller
348. Reflect or recall
349. Regulate things
350. Rehabilitate people
351. Rehabilitate things
352. Remember
353. Render or give support
354. Repair things
355. Repeat same task over and over
356. Report data, information
357. Represent people, organizations, or employers
358. Reproduce, duplicate, or copy materials
359. Reproduce sounds
360. Research
361. Reshape things
362. Restore or finish
363. Retrieve data, information, files
364. Review
365. Revise
366. Run or chair meetings or programs
367. Schedule own time or time of others
368. Screen applicants
369. Seize opportunities
370. Select items or products
371. Select people
372. Self-assessment
373. Sell
374. Sense moods or feelings
375. Sense the needs of others
376. Sequence tasks or flow chart processes
377. Serve people
378. Service equipment
379. Set criteria or standards of quality
380. Set goals and objectives
381. Set Limits
382. Set up equipment
383. Set up systems, services, or programs
384. Sew clothing or other materials
385. Shape things
386. Ship items
387. Show confidence or courage
388. Signal
389. Simplify
390. Sing
391. Skate
392. Sketch
393. Ski
394. Solve problems
395. Sort data or information
396. Sort objects
397. Spatial perception or reasoning
398. Speed up jobs, projects, services
399. Statistics
400. Stimulate people
401. Straighten things
402. Strategy develoment
403. Strengthen objects or materials
404. Strengthen programs
405. Study
406. Style hair
407. Summarize
408. Supervise
409. Supply or stock items
410. Survey for information or opinions
411. Survey land
412. Swim
413. Synthesize
414. Systematize
415. Tabulate information or data
416. Be tactful
417. Take accurate measurements
418. Take initiative
419. Take instructions

420. Tend animals
421. Tend machines, equipment
422. Test
423. Think ahead
424. Tolerate interruptions, inconveniences
425. Tolerate routine or boring tasks
426. Track or monitor situations or information
427. Train, instruct, or teach
428. Transcribe
429. Transfer data or information
430. Transfer things from one place to another
431. Translate
432. Travel in unknown territories
433. Troubleshoot
434. Tune machines, equipment
435. Tune musical instruments
436. Tutor
437. Type, use keyboard
438. Understand behavior
439. Understand cause and effect relationships
440. Understand or interpret information
441. Unite or get people working together
442. Upgrade quality
443. Use keen physical sensations
444. Use keen sense of rhythm
445. Use keen sense of smell
446. Use keen sense of timing
447. Use keen sense of touch
448. Use sophisticated equipment, instruments
449. Use personal contacts, networks
450. Use physical ability and agility
451. Use physical stamina
452. Verify information
453. Visualize ideas
454. Walk animals
455. Wash
456. Weave
457. Win friends and supporters
458. Work under stress
459. Work with animals
460. Work with precision
461. Wrap or package things
462. Write creative fiction, nonfiction
463. Write proposals
464. Write technical materials

★ **Step 3** Review each double-check-marked ✓✓ skill. Then highlight with a colored marker the top 20 transferable skills that best support your job entry.

★ **Step 4** Copy this information onto your job offer generator grid on page 21.

Career Vocabulary

A career vocabulary is made up of the words associated with a particular career field. Proper use of these terms reflects your knowledge of that field.

Using these words correctly can get you past the gatekeepers and is the best way to show the interviewer that you have a firm understanding of the job skills required for the job. A fluent career vocabulary is vital to your job search and will make you virtually screen-proof.

Also, by using the vocabulary of the field in your cover letters, resumes, and interviews, you're constantly reinforcing your job knowledge.

• Develop Your Career Vocabulary

There are a couple of easy methods for building up a powerful, screen-proof career vocabulary. Each of them requires you to analyze your work and education history, previous job functions, and the position you're seeking.

Government Publications One quick and dirty method to develop your career vocabulary is to use government publications. Let your Uncle Sam and your tax money help you identify the skills required for the job you want, so you can convince the employer you know what you're supposed to be doing for a living.

The *Dictionary of Occupational Titles* (Washington, D.C.: U.S. Government Printing Office) gives the most important skills needed to do the job and should jump start your memory. We advise going to your employment office or library and asking them for help using it.

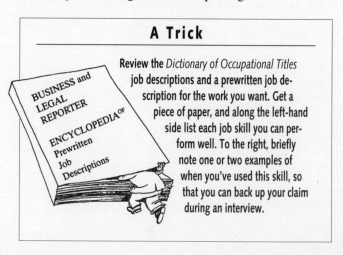

A Trick

Review the *Dictionary of Occupational Titles* job descriptions and a prewritten job description for the work you want. Get a piece of paper, and along the left-hand side list each job skill you can perform well. To the right, briefly note one or two examples of when you've used this skill, so that you can back up your claim during an interview.

The Drafting Profession:
A Couple of Related Job Descriptions from the Dictionary of Occupational Titles

DRAFTER, CIVIL (profess. & kin.) alternate titles: drafter, civil engineer; drafter, construction; drafter, engineering

Drafts detailed construction drawings, topographical profiles, and related maps and specifications used in planning and construction of civil engineering projects, such as highways, river and harbor improvements, flood control and drainage: Reviews rough sketches, drawings, specifications, and other engineering data. Plots maps and charts showing profiles and cross-sections, indicating relation of topographical contours and elevations to buildings, retaining walls, tunnels, overhead power lines, and other structures. Drafts detailed drawings of structures and installations, such as roads, culverts, fresh water supply, sewage disposal systems, dikes, wharves, and breakwaters. Computes volume of tonnage of excavations and fills and prepares graphs and hauling diagrams used in earthmoving operations. Performs other duties as described under DRAFTER (profess. & kin.) Master Title. May accompany survey crew in field to locate grading markers or to collect data required for revision of construction drawings. May specialize in drafting and modifying topographical maps from surveying notes and aerial photographs and be designated Drafter, Topographical (profess. & kin.) May use computer-assisted drafting (CAD) equipment and software and be designated Drafter, Civil (CAD) (profess. & kin.)

DESIGN TECHNICIAN, COMPUTER-AIDED (electron. comp.) alternate titles: digitizer

Operates computer-aided design (CAD) system and peripheral equipment to re-size or modify integrated circuit designs (artwork) and to generate computer tape of artwork for use in producing mask plates used in manufacturing integrated circuits. Reviews work order and procedural manuals to determine critical dimensions of design. Calculates figures to convert design dimensions to resizing dimensions specified for subsequent production processes, using conversion chart and calculator. Locates file relating to specified design projection data base library and loads program into computer. Enters specified commands into computer, using keyboard, to retrieve design information from file and display design on CAD equipment display screen. Types commands on keyboard to enter resizing specifications into computer. Confers with engineering and design staff to determine design modifications and enters editing information into computer. Keys in specified information, using keyboard connected to on-line or off-line peripheral equipment (plotter), to produce graphic representation (hard copy) of design for review and approval by engineering and design staff. Enters specified information into computer, using keyboard, to generate computer tape of approved design.

Prewritten Job Descriptions Prewritten job descriptions provide an almost magical way to define your job-related skills and improve your career vocabulary. They also will tell you a lot about other screening and matching factors considered important to most employers. The *Encyclopedia of Prewritten Job Descriptions* (Madison, CT : Business and Legal Reports, Inc., 1994; (203) 245-7448) is an excellent source.

How Can You Get These Job Descriptions?

1. Contact people you know who do the type of work you want to do or call a human resource professional who hires people in the field, and ask them for help getting a job description.

2. Try to get this information from your job service or Job Training Partnership Act (JTPA) organization (see page 86).

3. Buy a whole book of prewritten job descriptions from Business and Legal Reports by calling (203) 245-7448.

4. Give us a call at Job Search Training Systems at (800) 361-1613. We can probably be of some help.

• The Three Main Job Functions

What will you do in your next job? No matter what type of work you're looking for, you'll function and interact in your job in three ways. Everyone works with some kind of **data**, they're involved with **people**, and they operate some type of **tool, machine, or equipment**. The best way to develop your career vocabulary is by analyzing the job you want against these labor market standards. When you can complete these two pages, you're ready to look for work!

JOB SUMMARY:
Draftsman, Layout, Class "A" (from the
Encyclopedia of Prewritten Job Descriptions)

Lays out complete products and prepares assembly and detail drawings, following the general instructions and directions of a designer. Makes various calculations such as strength of materials, weights, simple forces, and stresses, frequently using charts and tables. Prepares bills of material and specifications. The incumbent reports to the R&D Engineer or Engineering Manager.

DUTIES AND RESPONSIBILITIES:

1. Prepares layouts, assembly, and detail drawings for new or improved products, special machinery design, test equipment, tools, fixtures, and gauge design.

2. Prepares initial drawings on designated test apparatus and monitors results.

3. Assists in the follow-up of prototype construction with outside vendors. Secures quotations and expedites materials and delivery.

4. Analyzes various design requirements and recommends possible solutions or alternate constructions. Also prepares and evaluates tolerance stack-ups. Provides information when required for cost estimating, such as blank layouts and processing sketches.

5. Makes orthographic or isometric illustrations required for sales aids.

EDUCATION AND EXPERIENCE

1. One (1) to two (2) years college or trade school education in mechanical drawing and related areas is helpful.

2. Well-rounded, practical experience may be substituted for formal training.

3. Able to move from design concept to finished design, including layouts and valuations and detail drawings.

4. Minimum five (5) years on-the-job experience.

MANAGERIAL SKILLS

(Numbers indicate which skills are of (1) primary importance, (2) secondary importance, (3) beneficial but not required, or (4) not required for this position.)

Controlling - 4	Developing subordinates - 4
Courage to act - 4	Motivating employees - 4
Ability to delegate - 4	Working under pressure - 3
Organizing - 3	Communicating, written - 3
Judgment - 1	Communicating, orally - 2
Planning - 2	Drive and initiative - 2
Flexibility - 2	Creativity - 1
Cooperation - 1	Accuracy - 1
Timeliness - 1	

Must be cost conscious, mechanically inclined, and able to use ingenuity and imagination to innovatively solve design and production problems.

Data Functions Data is any type of factual information, including anything you have to count or measure. Most everyone creates or uses some type of data or information in their work.

★ What types of data will you work with, use, or create in that position?

_____
_____
_____
_____
_____
_____
_____
_____
_____
_____

★ What will you do with this data?

_____
_____
_____
_____
_____
_____
_____
_____
_____
_____
_____

★ Workers perform seven basic functions with data:

Synthesize

Coordinate

Analyze

Compile

Compute

Copy

Compare

People Functions Every job in America requires some level of involvement with people: customers, coworkers, subordinates, supervisors, vendors/salespeople, etc.

★ What types of people will you regularly come in contact with?

_____
_____
_____
_____
_____
_____
_____
_____
_____
_____

★ What will you do with these people, to them, or for them?

_____
_____
_____
_____
_____
_____
_____
_____
_____
_____
_____
_____
_____

★ These are nine primary people-oriented tasks:

Mentoring

Negotiating

Instructing

Supervising

Entertaining

Persuading

Speaking

Serving

Taking instructions

Tool, Machine, and Equipment Functions Every job in America requires some involvement with tools, machines, or equipment.

★ What types of equipment will you operate on the job?

_____
_____
_____
_____
_____
_____
_____
_____
_____
_____

★ What will you do with this equipment?

_____
_____
_____
_____
_____
_____
_____
_____
_____
_____
_____

★ These are eight primary tool, machine, and equipment functions:

Designing and setting up

Performing precision work

Operating

Driving

Manipulating

Tending and maintaining

Feeding and off-loading

Handling machines and materials

Take the 20 words or phrases that best demonstrate your career knowledge and enter them in your job offer generator grid, page 21.

What Sets You Apart from the Competition

Now that you've spent some time with our exercises and identified your job skills, your people skills, and your transferable skills, you're well ahead of the game. But to really stand apart from your fellow job seekers, take a little more time and think of some of your special abilities.

• Special Knowledge

Most good jobs require some type of specialized skill or training. What about the kind of job you want—will you need to have any special skills? Do you have these skills now? Name them.

_____

_____

_____

_____

_____

_____

_____

_____

_____

If you don't have the requisite special knowledge, are you willing to work to acquire it? How?

• Problem-Solving Ability

Every employer wants workers who can solve problems and come up with safety, money, and time-saving ideas. What types of problems do you think you would have to solve to get ahead in your field?

_____

_____

_____

_____

_____

_____

_____

_____

_____

_____

Send $4.95 and we'll do all of the hard work for you. Our address is on page 86. We have a number of different career vocabularies available for the job titles listed on pages 77–80.

If your job title isn't listed, give us a call. We have others!

Job Offer Generator Grid
Your Skills at a Glance

List your 20 top fitting-in skills from your exercise (page 9)	**List your 20 top transferable skills from your exercise (page 11–16)**	**List your 20 top words from your career vocabulary (pages 18–19)**
1.	1.	1.
2.	2.	2.
3.	3.	3.
4.	4.	4.
5.	5.	5.
6.	6.	6.
7.	7.	7.
8.	8.	8.
9.	9.	9.
10.	10.	10.
11.	11.	11.
12.	12.	12.
13.	13.	13.
14.	14.	14.
15.	15.	15.
16.	16.	16.
17.	17.	17.
18.	18.	18.
19.	19.	19.
20.	20.	20.

5 Research Information

How to Analyze Jobs, the Companies, and Hiring Practices

We know that most interviewers give you points for knowing about the company, the job, and the problems associated with people working in the field. We also know that the best way to get information about a company's needs, concerns, and hiring practices is to ask the people doing the hiring!

We strongly advise that you research the policies of at least six different employers in the line of work you're pursuing. You'll see a pattern evolve, and this information will be of immense help as you prepare for your interviews.

We don't think you're ready to look for work unless you have the information provided by this exercise.

How to Set Up Research Time

It's okay to do research by phone, but you will benefit much more from a face-to-face meeting with a hiring authority. It's also okay to just drop by unannounced. It's even okay to take a friend (but only *one*) if you're nervous.

Believe it or not, the best time to do this has proven to be between 3:00 and 5:00 P.M.

How to Introduce Yourself

Follow our script! It's okay to change our words and inject your own style, but keep to the theme and the goal.

I'm not looking for work today, but I'm beginning a career/job [choose one] change and would like to ask for five minutes of your time to answer some research questions I have about your field.

My purpose for being here [calling] is that I'm looking for people who really know this field and figure department heads and managers are the best folks to talk to.

My goal is to get enough new information about the field so that when I start looking for work I'll be able to show how I can be a profitable and productive worker.

Research Rule

Asking the right people the right questions
is always the best way to get answers.

Company research sheds light on...

- Job performance criteria
- Time and pressure demands
- Skill requirements
- Educational demands
- Hiring practices

**and should always be done before
your job search and interview!**

Questions to Ask

You will want to ask about job performance criteria, skill requirements, time and work pressures, educational demands, and hiring practices. We've prepared these questions for you, so you can make copies of these pages and use them as your worksheet when you're doing your research.

- **Questions to Ask about Job Performance**

1. In what department/unit/division would a person with my skills usually work? What would be their job title? [Give them a copy of your job offer generator grid (page 21) or your self-marketing skills card (page 31) for review. This question implies that you have completed your job offer generator grid. If you haven't you're not ready to do this exercise.]

   _____

   _____

   _____

   _____

2. What behaviors do the supervisors reward most often? What is the usual method of reward?

   _____

   _____

   _____

   _____

3. What's the biggest problem these supervisors have with the people who work for them?

    _____
    _____
    _____
    _____

4. What are the determining factors for advancement and raises?

    _____
    _____
    _____
    _____

• Questions to Ask about Time and Work Pressures

1. How much travel, overtime, and holiday work can be expected?

    _____
    _____
    _____
    _____

2. How much notice is usually given?

    _____
    _____
    _____
    _____

• Questions to Ask about Skill Requirements

1. What five skills are most important for success in this field?

    _____
    _____
    _____
    _____

2. What five personality traits are the most critical for success?

    _____
    _____
    _____
    _____
    _____

3. What are the three biggest problems the workers say they have with this type of work and with getting their job done?

    _____
    _____
    _____
    _____

4. Have you ever hired someone who didn't have all of the experience requested? What did they do to convince you?

    _____
    _____
    _____
    _____

• Questions to Ask about Educational Demands

1. What education requirements must be met to be successful in this field?

    _____
    _____
    _____

2. What ongoing education or on-the-job training is needed?

    _____
    _____
    _____
    _____

• Questions to Ask about Hiring Practices

1. What's the toughest question you ask people in the interview, and how would you like to have it answered?

    _____
    _____
    _____
    _____

2. What's your opinion of resumes? What do you want to see on them, and what don't you like?

_____

_____

_____

_____

3. What's the biggest problem you see on application forms?

_____

_____

_____

_____

4. What are your biggest concerns when interviewing someone for this type of work?

_____

_____

_____

_____

A Word of Caution

Call for information about the company's products and services before attempting this exercise.

A Networking Trick Ask these two questions last:

1. Can you give me the names of two other people with whom I can talk who are as knowledgeable in this field as you are?

2. Is it okay if I keep in touch as my search progresses?

(More about networking in Chapter 8.)

Now you've got yourself into the right mind-set, figured out what you want from a job and what you can give to an employer, and done some research that will put you way out ahead of the competition. Before we start building your job search tools and skills, here are a few insider's tips about the screening process.

The Screening Process

During everyone's job search there are at least three different stages at which you might get trapped by a "gatekeeper"—this could be the boss's secretary, a personnel clerk, initial resume reviewer, or even a recruiter. The gatekeeper's objective is to keep lesser qualified applicants from getting to the "hiring authority" and receiving a job offer.

Gatekeepers use a variety of methods to screen you in (or out of) the selection and hiring process. So you need a variety of different methods to get past them.

By knowing how gatekeepers screen people in or out, you can reduce the risk of eliminating yourself from the running right at the start of the race.

• How Do You Get Your Foot in the Door?

The first gatekeeper's job is to let in the applicants who most closely match the employer's hiring criteria—and keep out the others. The tools they use are your

★ application forms

★ cover letters

★ resumes

They weigh the information you provide against their hiring and qualification criteria and a detailed job summary. This information is commonly summarized in a prewritten job description, or an employee recruitment order, and generally covers:

★ essential job functions (duties and responsibilities)

★ educational requirements

★ critical skills and knowledge

★ required experience

★ supervision levels

★ personality traits desired

★ physical requirements

★ salary range

If the preliminary information you present in your application, cover letter, and resume does not match up pretty well against the company's requirements, your chances of moving to the next screening level, the interview, aren't good.

One of the best ways to insure that you're not blown out of the water in the first round of screening is to *develop your career vocabulary* for the position (see pages 16–20) and use that vocabulary at every opportunity!

Can You Keep Your Application from Trashing You?

• How Do You Keep Your Foot in the Door?

The second gatekeeper is the digger of information—the interviewer. Sometimes there's more than one. These folks want to verify if you, the candidate, can

★ really do the job

★ fit into the company

★ add to the company

Their tools are

★ telephone screening test

★ interview questions

★ reference checking

The interview is a very important part of the employee selection process since over 40 percent of the people who get fired are unloaded for incompetency. These people just don't do their job very well. Having to fire someone for incompetency is costly to the employer—and doesn't make the interviewer look too hot!

• How Do You Get Your Whole Body to Follow Your Foot?

The last gatekeeper—your last hurdle—is usually the second or third interviewer, and the final decision maker.

Now your employment soul is up for grabs.

The employer knows you can do the job, or you wouldn't have gotten this far. Now you're in personality competition with just a few folks—not the thundering hordes.

How will you set yourself apart from the competition?

★ Send thank-you notes to everyone

★ Recontact them with more questions

★ Call to give them more information

★ Drop by with recommendation letters or other support showing your value as a worker

★ Ask for a tour of the company and the location where you'd be working

Every little bit can help you get the job offer!

6 Job Search Tools

Power Up Your Applications, Cover Letters, and Resumes

These are the tools that will get you past that first gatekeeper—make them good! Application forms are a necessary evil of the employment process—and have one of the lowest rates of success of any job search tool. But, since virtually everyone looking for work will have to fill at least one out...

Here are a few ways to make your application stand out from the competition.

• Position Desired

Always specify a job objective and add "or a related position." This broadens your job objective and opens the door for other opportunities, even if they're not hiring your job title.

• Salary Requirements

Get attention! Instead of writing "negotiable" or "open":

★ **Use a range.** But know what that range should be by getting the prevailing wages in your area.

★ **Dare to be different.** Write "based on responsibilities" or "based on skills and abilities used in the job."

★ **And be careful.** If you put a dollar amount in this area, you can be too high . . . and be screened out. Or, you can be too low. . . and be screened out.

• Describe Former Duties and Responsibilities

Here are a couple of easy tricks that will make you stand out!

★ Review your **career vocabulary** and try to use as many of the words as you can to show you've performed similar work and used similar skills.

★ Indicate any achievement, awards, raises, or bonuses for superior work—even if there's no place for it. Make room in the margin, tag it with post-it notes, or add an extra sheet to the application. You're trying to be remembered!

Don't Get Caught in the Application Trap

Good applications are

- neat
- complete
- accurate
- honest
- informative
- helpful to employers

Good applications link

- life experiences
- education and training
- military experiences
- volunteer experiences
- work experiences
- successes and achievements

to the position you want

Good applications minimize

- health problems
- school problems
- marital problems
- legal problems
- financial problems
- interpersonal problems
- job retention problems

Good applications

- specify position desired
- power up salary section
- indicate future goals
- explain work history gaps
- present related skills
- power up education section
- power up work history section
- screen you *into* interviews

• Dates of Employment

If you've held a job for less than three months, you probably don't want to include it, unless it's one that directly supports your ability to do the job. And remember, employers aren't fools. They know that a lot of people try to cover brief or unsuccessful work experiences by using only the year as the date. So be specific and always use the month and year here.

• Previous Job Title or Position Held

Instead of just listing your title, spice up the section by showing growth with this type of attention-getting technique: *Promoted from carpenter to interior trim lead person.*

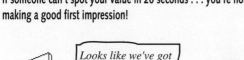

The 20-Second Cover Letter Success Rule

If someone can't spot your value in 20 seconds . . . you're not making a good first impression!

Remember the Three-Line Rule:

If it takes more than three lines to say, maybe it's not worth saying.

Cover Letters

Of the many different types of cover letters you could learn to create, our experience shows that the KISS (Keep It So Simple) type of cover letter is your best bet.

• Why the KISS Letter Is the Best

★ It's probably the easiest type of cover letter for you to create—and the easiest for the employer to read. If you just follow the general format tips, you can't go wrong.

★ It's easily adapted to different jobs and companies—certainly more adaptable than "gimmicky" letters.

★ Most important, every word in it focuses on our three rules of cover letter success:
    1. Talk about your relevant skills.
    2. Show that you meet the employer's needs.
    3. Give proof of your skills and value.

• Cover Letter Rules of Thumb

★ Limit letter to one page.

★ Limit content to six sections.

★ Limit each section to six lines or less.

★ Use $8\frac{1}{2}$-by-11-inch white bond paper.

★ Set $\frac{3}{4}$-inch to 1-inch margins.

★ Have three people proofread it to make sure there are no spelling or grammar mistakes.

★ Customize: never use a form letter.

★ Be assertive, write with confidence.

★ Present only facts that you can back up.

★ *Don't include* letters of recommendation, transcripts, or reference lists unless requested.

For more information on the different styles of cover letters, we recommend *Dynamic Cover Letters* by Katharine Hansen (Berkeley, CA: Ten Speed Press, 1995).

KISS Cover Letter Development

If you don't know who you are, maybe you shouldn't be looking for work!

Always target a real person. Find the name and title of the department head, manager, boss.

Dare to be different and get attention!

Section 1: Get to the point, specify what you want, show some enthusiasm, and state how you found out about this career opportunity!

Section 2: State how much experience you have and where you got it (life, work, or education). List any reinforcing education, on-the-job training, or seminars. Include GPA *only* if "B" or higher!

KISS Rule #1

Solid content is more important than creativity!

KISS Rule #2

Always make sure your cover letter addresses every point listed in a Help Wanted ad!

KISS Rule #3

Never use a form letter. Each letter should be individually written!

Elvira J. Shagnasty
1214 N. Euclid
Nineveh, IN 46164
(317) 435-1234

April 1, 1995

Ms. Miranda Hill
Credit Manager
AAA Leasing, Inc.
122 Finance Parkway
Indianapolis, IN 46235-1098

A Very Good Day Ms. Hill,

I'm more than a little interested in the accounts manager position that
    ...was listed in Sunday's *Star*.
    ...Tom Adams told me you might be looking to fill.
    ...we talked about yesterday on the phone.

I have a three-year track record of successful work and educational experience. I've earned an AAS Accounting degree (3.56 GPA) and have successfully completed a number of management and on-the-job-training seminars. I can:

- track payables and receivables
- review and analyze cash flow
- prepare financial statements
- generate payroll information
- coordinate year-end audit review for tax purposes
- utilize a variety of computer accounting packages
- monitor, write, and call past due accounts for collection
- train and oversee the work of other accounting clerks

I'm proud to say that I've received achievement awards, pats-on-the-back, or bonuses for:

- collecting 30% more outstanding receivables than my predecessor and;
- reducing, by 10%, the time needed to complete in-house forms and;
- restructuring the payables department which saved $5,000 in late payment fees.

Other transferable skills I have which support my ability to be a productive worker for you include:

- planning and scheduling
- identifying and solving problems
- organization
- utilizing time efficiently
- budget management
- high energy
- decision making
- team orientation

I'd like to thank you for the time and consideration and close by saying that I have the skills and desire to do a good job for you. I'm loyal to my employer and I'm seriously interested in a career. I'll contact your office in a couple of days to insure receipt of my resume and schedule a time when we can talk.

Sincerely,

Elvira J. Shagnasty

Elvira J. Shagnasty

Enclosure[s]: Resume
             Portfolio [if appropriate]

Use bullets (•) for emphasis and reading ease!

Indicate a point of pride.

If you're a graduating student without much work experience, list your school or life-related successes!

Don't space out! Call them in two or three days and schedule an interview.

Section 3: Identify the most important skills required for the job sought and match them to your own. Get this information from:

- your career vocabulary exercise (pages 16-20)
- prewritten job descriptions
- the *Dictionary of Occupational Titles*

If you're a graduating student or without much work experience, during the interview you'll have to talk about how your life/education taught you to use these skills.

Section 4: List *any* relevant and provable achievements or successes that might ring the employer's bell and show you can do the job!

Section 5: List up to eight of your transferable skills and personality traits from your job offer generator grid (page 21).

Section 6: Close with some power! Make a personal commitment to the reader! Stress career orientation, loyalty, and willingness to do quality work. Take charge—don't wimp out:

- Define your next step.
- State when you'll contact them.
- Never use the words: "job" or "interview."
- Always ask for a time to meet.

Resumes

What do we know about resumes?

• How to Create a Screen-Proof Resume

1. The resume is a screening device. The odds of the average resume generating a job offer is about 8 percent (Bolles, *What Color is Your Parachute?* 1994, Berkeley, CA: Ten Speed Press). With a well-thought-out resume, you can beat those odds and win the resume race.

2. A resume is a closed system. You only have so much space to prove you have the skills, abilities, and experience for the position. Use every inch to promote your value as an employee.

3. The best resume is a combination, targeted resume. "Combination" means that you both list your work history and highlight the key skills you can bring to the job. This style overcomes a problem encountered by many employers. A good many people try to hide limited work experience, job hopping, job gaps, or termination by eliminating the dates and companies for which they've worked and only presenting their key skills to the employer. This type of "no history" resume is called a functional resume. The word "targeted" implies that the resume is created for a specific job—and most desirably for a specific company. It not only targets your key skills but focuses on the results of your using these skills. It also shows the employer that you've put in the time to analyze your skills and is a strong indicator of the effort you've expended to research the company and meet their needs, better supporting your entry into the position. The combination, targeted resume works because it avoids the most common resume mistakes and focuses on the issues of most concern to the people who will be reviewing it.

• What Employers Look For

What do employers look for when screening resumes?

1. **A match** They want to see whether your work history, knowledge and skills, education, training, and achievements will match their needs.

2. **Positive patterns** They look for a logical progression from one job to another with a reasonable amount of time per job, promotions, awards, and other good results.

3. **Positive indicators** They look for favorable personality traits, work habits, and interpersonal skills, as well as loyalty and successful project completion.

4. **Knockouts** They look for any simple, clear-cut facts that immediately put the person out of the running, such as: inability or unwillingness to relocate, inappropriate education or experience, inappropriate salary demands, and not avoiding common resume mistakes, like those listed below.

Adapted from *How to Review Resumes* (Madison, CT: Business and Legal Reports, Inc., 1986; (203) 245-7448)

• Avoid These Common Resume Mistakes

★ Too slick (it's obviously not done by you)

★ Career/job objective is missing or unrealistic

★ Information isn't relevant to the job

★ Wordy, vague, unfocused, rambling

★ Focuses on duties rather than responsibilities

★ Lacks performance results—concrete ways your employers benefited from your skills

★ Gives no examples of achievements or success—awards and promotions

★ Lacks hard numbers to back up achievements

★ Work history is spotty, fraudulent, or missing

★ Education is overemphasized

★ Experience is all equally billed

★ Crucial skills are buried and hard to find

★ Layout is too difficult to read quickly

★ Typos, poor grammar, misspelling

KISS Resume —Combination, Targetted Style

State career objective

- Specify the type of work you're seeking.
- Expand your opportunities by including "or a related position."
- Include one or two of your best personality traits.

Skill and duties summary

List up to six of the most common daily duties in this type of work setting and use bullets for emphasis.

Use bullets for emphasis

Highlight items in a list with bullets (★, •, or other type).

List key responsibilities

List up to 10 key responsibilities that are critical to this position and that you can link up to your life, work, or educational experiences.

Group similar responsibilities together.

Stress related experience.

- Company name only (no address) is okay!
- Years of employment (no month) are okay!

Highlight education.

- Target highest educational level.
- List any other relevant education.

Close with power!

Make a personal statement about yourself and your work.

Frank Johnson
(317) 933-3961

941 North Cherry Street
Indianapolis, IN 46202

• **Career Objective** •

A warehouse management or related position in a company desiring a conscientious, hard-working person with the following skills.

★ Receiving/shipping	★ Transportation
★ Order filling	★ Scheduling
★ Maintaining stock records	★ Coordinating worker activities

• **Reinforceable Accomplishments** •

Supervision and Training

★ Supervised and instructed 30–60 employees in warehouse operational procedures and policies with outstanding results. Grievances and employee turnover both dropped by 95 percent.

★ Increased my department's productivity by training "less than motivated" day laborers in more efficient material-handling methods.

Interpersonal and Problem Solving

★ Strong and proven capabilities managing crisis events such as the need to reschedule, reroute, or alter common carrier to provide more expeditious delivery of products.

★ Can effectively communicate with all levels of personnel—management, union, and employees—thus facilitating smoother, more harmonious work atmosphere. This translates into less friction, higher efficiency, and cost savings in the thousands of dollars.

Inventory Management and Organization

★ Reorganized $6 million inventory in a 100,000-sq.-ft. public warehouse that shipped locally, nationally, and internationally. Reorganization yielded quicker delivery time, less driver "wait" time, and more ease of retrieval and transport of stock merchandise.

★ Successful at handling, shipping, and receiving over 20,000 items per day with virtually no loss, damage, or failure of delivery.

Savings and Loss Prevention

★ Generated a new income source of $2 million per six months by finding a resale outlet for scrap materials that were originally discarded at a cost to the employer.

★ Designed and implemented a loss prevention program that reduced losses by $1,400 per month.

Common Carrier Liaison

★ Excellent working relationship with over 35 common carriers. Well versed in the use of common carriers, air freight, and UPS materials transportation processes and in how each system can be utilized for best results.

Safety Conscious

★ Solely responsible for monitoring required safety training program for eight forklift drivers, resulting in 20 percent reduction in injuries (no injuries in nine months).

• **Related Work Experience** •

Indy Warehousing	1989–present	Stacker, forklift driver, night supervisor
Caito Shipping	1985–1989	Loader, team leader
J.C. Penney	1984–1985	Stock clerk (part time while in school)

• **Relevant Education** •

AAS Business Management   Indiana Vocational Tech   (3.4 GPA)

• **Relevant on-the-job training and seminars** •

• Loss Prevention   • OSHA Safety Training   • Meeting ADA Regulations
• Total Quality Management

Career-minded, honest, dependable and
can be counted on to do quality work!

Balance your name, address, and phone number on the page.
This saves space, which can then be devoted to saying something about your value as a worker.

Give examples as proof.
For every "key responsibility" give at least one *successful* example of your performance.

Specify results.
What happened from your efforts? Use hard numbers if you're able.

Quantify.
Almost everything is measurable. Talk about dollar value, savings, size, volume, distance, quotas, percentages, frequency, lengths of time needed, etc. This information gives employers something solid with which to compare your resume against less well-prepared ones.

Show advancement.
Stress growth in positions held while at each company.

• Design Tips

If you don't have a word processor, then for heaven's sake, go out and find someone with one. Save your time and maintain your sanity.

★ **Length** Usually 1 page is enough, 2 maximum!

★ **Paper** $8\frac{1}{2}$-by-11-inches, good white bond to match cover letter, with matching envelope

★ **Ink** Black or dark blue (makes a striking appearance on white paper)

★ **Typeface** Stick to one typeface throughout. Times is a good choice.

★ **Type Size** If you have less information to present, use a larger point size—10 point minimum, 12 point maximum.

★ **Justification** Justify the left margin and leave ragged edges on the right. It's easier to read.

★ **Margins** $\frac{3}{4}$ inch to 1 inch. Use wider margins if you have less material.

★ **Boldface** Your name and address, each major section, and key skills should be emphasized in bold print.

For comprehensive information on different styles of resumes, we recommend any of Yana Parker's resume books, published by Ten Speed Press.

The Skills Summary Card

The skills summary card is a self-marketing business card. It's a unique job search tool designed to highlight your experience, skills, education, and related achievements.

• Why It Works

It's small but powerful! It summarizes what you have to offer an employer while demonstrating your innovative approach to job seeking. Simple and easy-to-read, this little card will catch many an eye and will help people remember you, your skills, and your successes.

Sample Skills Summary Card

Bolivar J. Shagnasty

Career Objective

Accounting Manager
Or Similar Position

(317) 933-3961

Front (folded)

Experience: Over three years of directly related experience.

Job-related skills:
• tracking payables/receivables, reporting significant issues
• reviewing and analyzing cash flow, and insuring accuracy
• preparing financial statements, generating payroll data
• coordinating year-end audit review for tax purposes
• using computerized spreadsheet/accounting packages
• monitoring past due accounts, writing and calling for collection

— — — — — — — — — — — — — — — — — — fold

Transferable Skills:
• planning projects
• communicating
• managing budgets
• supervisory skills
• identifying & solving problems
• utilizing time effectively
• training and developing others
• making critical decisions

Self-management skills:
• high energy
• accurate
• analytical
• responsible
• team player
• productive

Inside (opened)

Achievements:
• collected 30 percent more outstanding receivables
• reduced by 10 percent the time needed to complete forms
• coordinated departments and saved $5,000 in late fees

Related education:
• Graduate, Management Training Program (3.5 GPA)
• Associates Degree, Accounting (3.56 GPA)

Back (folded) Optional

• How to Use It

1. Hand out a few cards when you meet people and ask them to pass one on to someone they know (or someone who knows someone) in the field you're interested in. Don't think you're being pushy or imposing—it's normal for people to give and receive business cards!

2. Set yourself apart and impress interviewers by giving them your job seeker's business card as you prepare to close the interview. Ask them to place it on your application and resume package—and they *will* remember you!

3. Give a card to anyone you plan to use as a reference. People often have trouble defining someone else's skills. Help them help you!

4. Make sure all the people and agencies helping you find work get a card. In fact, give them an extra one to pass on. This includes job service offices, your school placement office, outplacement and employment agencies, Job Training Partnership centers (see page 86), your family and friends, bartenders, hair stylists, postal delivery people, church and club members—or anyone else that comes into public contact.

5. When you hear, "We're not taking applications or resumes," give out one of your cards instead.

• Design Issues: Keep It Simple

★ **Typeface** Times (easy to read), 10 point or bigger

★ **Paper** Regular business-card stock

★ **Graphics** If you can find one that relates to your line of work, clip it out and use it.

★ **Content** Select your most relevant skills and successes from your skills identification exercises, prewritten job descriptions, job research exercises, and the *Dictionary of Occupational Titles*. (Keep it brief—you're not writing a book, I am!)

Phone fear = fewer interviews!

Phone Contact Script

The odds are really against job seekers who only use applications and resumes to make contact. By learning to develop and follow up on job leads by phone you radically improve your odds of getting the interview—in our experience, by over 100 percent. The first steps are:

1. to not hide from one of the most important job search tools you have

2. to develop a basic phone script

• Why This Approach Is So Important

Using the phone allows you to:

★ make personal contact with a hiring authority—which can breed many more interviews

★ make many employer contacts in a day

★ break the monotony of shuffling papers all day

★ better use your network contacts and information

★ be in more control of your search activity

★ present your skills in a very brief period

★ do a prescreening interview—just the way bosses do

★ expand your network of people who know your skills and that you're looking for work

★ give a powerful first impression

★ look any way you want to!

• **Turn Your Skills Summary Card into a Phone Script**

The following is a sample phone script. You can easily make your own script from your skills summary card. The best script is a short one—keep it under a minute. Remember, less is more!

The phone: a direct line to more interviews and job offers

Elements of a Phone Script

1. Call the hiring authority.	1. Good afternoon, Mr. Poobah.
2. Identify yourself.	2. My name's Bolivar Shagnasty.
3. Specify who referred you (if appropriate) and indicate reason for the call.	3. An acquaintance of yours, Mr. Jones, was kind enough to pass on your name. He said you knew a lot about this field and that you might be willing to talk with me. I'm interested in a position as a bookkeeper.
4. State experience level.	4. I have over three years of directly related experience.
5. Define your job skills. Select the most powerful skills and traits from your skills summary card.	5. • I track payables and receivables and report significant issues. • I review and analyze cash flow and insure accuracy. • I can prepare financial statements and generate payroll data. • I collected 30 percent more outstanding receivables. • I have an associates degree in accounting (3.4 GPA). • I am high energy, responsible, accurate, and a team player.
6. Request an interview. Counter any rejections (see chapters 5 and 8 for all the help you'll need).	6. When would be a good time for me to come by and talk to you.
7. No interview? Get two referral names.	7. I'm sorry we can't get together. But would you be able to give me a couple of people's names who might be interested in a person with my skills?
8. Seek help and a critique.	8. Do you mind if I contact you again to see if you're making any personnel changes or to ask your advice?
9. Express thanks.	9. Thanks for your time.

The Odds Against Getting an Interview

300:1 — **Application**

254:1 — **Resume**

15:1 — **Telephone**

7 Interviewing
What Impresses (or Does Not Impress) Interviewers

Most interview mistakes are made because of a lack of understanding about what impresses the interviewers. Experience has proven that the best way to prepare yourself for an interview is to look at things from the employer's point of view:

★ What are they looking for?

★ How will they look for it?

Two studies by reputable companies in the personnel field give us an idea about how employers assess prospective candidates for jobs. Wonderlic is a respected personnel testing company. Table 7-1, "Predictors of Success," shows what their brochure tells their employer-clients about how to predict whether or not a person will be a successful employee. Pay special attention to the top four "predictors of success."

Table 7-1. Predictors of Success
(above .20 = best predictors)

Ability testing	.53
Job tryout	.44
Biographics (skills I.D.)	.37
Reference checking	.26
Experience	.18
Interviews	.14
Experience rating	.13
Academic achievement	.11
Educational background	.10
Interests	.10
Age	-.01

AccountTemps is a leading temporary employment agency. They did a survey of 1,000 employers to find out what employers valued most in an employee. Their findings are summarized in Table 7-2, "What Impresses Interviewers the Most." Enthusiasm and verbal skills get top billing—what should that say to you?

★ Learn to talk about your skills.

★ Get excited about yourself!

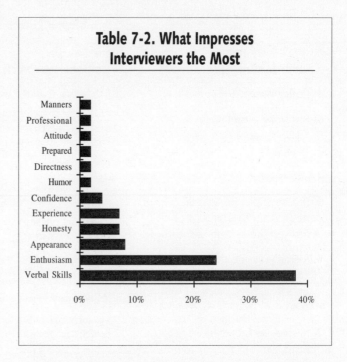

Table 7-2. What Impresses Interviewers the Most

These two charts tell us at least two important things. One, employers look very carefully at your job qualifications. Two, they also look at other things, such as appearance, the way you express yourself, your enthusiasm, and so forth.

• It's Not Just What You Say

Employers don't just listen to *what* you say—they also listen to *how* you say it. The Jacoby Voice Development Company reports that employers respond negatively to certain types of voices and styles of speech (see Table 7-3, "Negative Speech Characteristics."). Employers also pay close attention to what you *do*. You may not be aware of how much your "body language" can tell an interviewer about you. For example, looking down and not making eye contact are usually interpreted as lack of confidence. The same is true of a weak handshake. You also should avoid too *much* eye contact (staring), as well as those little fidgety movements that indicate nervousness, such as drumming your fingers or picking lint from your clothes!

Table 7-3.
Negative Speech Characteristics

Characteristic	Percent Disapproval
Whining	44.0%
Loud or grating	21.1%
High-pitched	15.9%
Mumbling	11.1%
Fast speech	4.9%
Unassertive	3.6%
Monotone	3.5%
Thick accent	2.4%

- **Avoid Common Mistakes (Keep Your Sneakers Out of Your Mouth at Interviews)**

Yes, there are lots of ways you can put your foot in your mouth. But don't worry—if you prepare yourself you can easily avoid these common mistakes.

Match Factors

We know that most interviewers look for a near-perfect match between the person, the job, and the company. They want to see if you have the traits and abilities to match the job. To determine this they look at a number of factors. Your goal is to learn to talk about and exhibit as many of these Match Factor Traits as possible.

★ **Good appearance** The way you look, speak, and act must all say: I can do the job.

★ **Friendliness, poise, and stability** Practice your interview skills, so that you can be cool (friendly and poised) under pressure. And be ready to give specific examples of getting along with supervisors, coworkers, and customers.

★ **Experience** Present only your most relevant experiences and talk about positive results.

Mistakes and How to Avoid Them

Mistake	How to Avoid It
Don't present your real self	Always be who you are. Employers spot fakes.
Try to play it by ear—wing it!	Know yourself, the job, and the company. Prepare. Don't be a fool.
Emphasize experiences before skills and value	Present your skills and value first, then back that up with experience.
Fail to present your relevant skills	Don't ramble. Talk only about your most relevant skills and successes.
Show no career orientation	Be ready to explain your next step up the career ladder.
Complain about prior employers	Don't! If you bad-mouth former employers, you'll be seen as likely to repeat the behavior.
Present vague answers	Answer questions fully and, when possible, with concrete examples.
Talk too much about too little	If you don't have something positive to say about your value, be quiet.
Don't talk the job vocabulary	Review your career vocabulary and use it when appropriate.
Don't present a complete picture of yourself	Show how your life, work, and educational experience can pay off for the employer.
Bring up negative personal information	Keep focused on the job duties—not your lifetime of woes and sorrows.

What two words have the most interview impact with younger managers and executives?

Dedication!
Teamwork!
Stress them!!

★ **Personality** Talk about how your personality fits the demands of the job and the company.

★ **Organization** Demonstrate your ability to be organized. Talk about one thing at a time, and answer questions with detailed examples.

★ **Motivation and attitude** Talk about what motivates you to do better than average work, and give examples of when you've gone above and beyond "the call of duty" to get the job done well.

★ **Expressiveness** Show your enthusiasm when you talk about your value and skills.

★ **Learning ability** Give examples of how well you've picked up new skills.

★ **Achievements** Back up your success stories with detailed proof. This way you're not bragging, just stating facts.

★ **Leadership** Tell about instances when you've had to take on more than just an employee's role.

★ **Skills** You must be able to identify your 60 most marketable skills (from your job offer generator grid, page 21)—or you're not job-search ready.

★ **Education** Can you tell the employer how your education has helped prepare you for this job?

★ **Test results** More and more companies are using ability testing, personality profiles, and drug tests to predict employment success. Can you pass the necessary academic and job skills test?

★ **Company knowledge** Explain what you've learned about the company—and how you found out about it.

★ **Symbiotic goals** Try to show how your skills, values, interests, and goals fit in with the needs of the company—how you and the company can form a mutually beneficial relationship.

★ **Decision making** Give examples of when you faced tough problems and had to make difficult choices to get the job done.

★ **Company loyalty** You want to be in a relationship that lasts and interviewers want people who want to stay with a company. How will you convince them of this?

★ **Promotability** The future's important. Describe yourself as a "go-getter," and discuss your plans for taking your next big career step.

★ **Altruism** Mention your volunteer activities. If you work for nothing to help other people, you'll probably be a more "giving" employee.

A Typical Interview

You've made it! You've gotten the interview and you're seated in the office of the interviewer. Now what happens? What's the normal flow of an interview? Generally interviewers follow a certain pattern:

They Socialize First they meet you, greet you, and small-talk you—no tough questions yet! They're trying to build rapport, make you comfortable, and reduce your anxiety. Let them! It makes them feel good and gives you a bit of time to collect yourself. Smile, show you're a member of the living, be excited—you've got an interview!

They Question At this point most applicants become part of the interviewer's food chain! The tough questions begin.

Although for certain occupations you may be asked additional types of questions, questions common to all fields will cover the following topics:

Initiative and motivation

Career ambitions and goals

Attendance and punctuality

Creativity and problem-solving skills

Organizational skills

Analytical skills

Attention to detail

Ability to learn

Flexibility

Interpersonal skills

Ability to resolve conflicts

Time and stress management

Who Gets the Second Interview?
People Who Exhibit These Traits and Talk about These Issues

• Appearance	• Career knowledge
• Friendliness	• Test results
• Poise, stability	• Company knowledge
• Experience	• Symbiotic goals
• Personality	• Achievements
• Organization	• Decision making
• Motivation	• Company loyalty
• Expressiveness	• Work attitude
• Learning ability	• Promotability
• Leadership	• Problem solving
• Skill match	• Retention factors
• Education match	• Volunteering

You Question Your turn up! This is the time when the interviewers ask: Do you have any questions?

Having no questions doesn't say much about your interest and alertness. Having irrelevant questions says even less.

Interview Success Rule #1

Every question you ask an interviewer should show your interest in moving up the career ladder and meeting company goals!

Good Questions Ask About . . .

- Job satisfaction
- Advancement
- Work environment
- Job specifications
- Financial compensation

They Inform If the interviewer likes what he or she has heard so far, she (or he) will begin to tell you more about the job, the company's policies and objectives, the people you'd work with, and so on.

Listen closely, and note any questions that come to mind. Also, if you pay attention you'll probably pick up clues as to what the company is really looking for in the new employee. This may give you the opportunity to match even more of your experiences to the employer's needs.

The questions you ask should show that you've listened attentively to the employer's needs, concerns, and questions. Good questions to ask the interviewer should focus on any of the following:

- ★ **Job specifications** (better define the position's duties and responsibilities)

- ★ **Job satisfaction** (be sure the position will motivate you to do good work)

- ★ **Work conditions** (understand, exactly, what you're in for—overtime, stress, people)

- ★ **Advancement** (make sure you know what's expected for upward mobility)

- ★ **Finances** (if there's a discrepancy between what you think you're worth and what they're saying they're willing to pay, find out why)

Interview Success Rule #2

Never leave the interview wihout telling the interviewer . . .

...I Want The Job!

...I'll Do Great Work!

...I Won't Let You Down!

And

- Schedule a call-back time
- Leave a skills summary card

They Define Their Next Move Now is when interviewers mentally stash you or trash you. If they still like you after your round of questions, they'll stash you in their memory and sell you on the job and let you know what the next step in the selection process will be. This usually includes scheduling you for a follow-up (second) interview—usually with someone else, or a group of someone elses. They may also schedule you for testing, background checks, physicals, and so forth. If you haven't measured up to their expectation, they'll begin the mental trashing process...immediately. (Get ready for the S^2—So Sorry—rejection letter.)

They Review Rarely will an interviewer tell you: "You've got the job!" on the first, or even the second, interview. He or she will want time to review your responses and compare you with the other applicants.

The first day or two after your interview is a great time to contact the interviewer again in order to reinforce your value, in any number of different ways—without becoming a pain in the butt or looking like a suck-up. It could be your last chance to affect the hiring decision!

Interview Success Rule #3

Always follow up

- Send thank-you notes
- Request additional information
- Ask well-thought-out questions

This is your last shot at getting the interviewer to remember you!

They Select and Reject Even though there are a myriad of factors that go into any hiring decision, there are four factors that are common to all of them—make them work for you!

1. Your personality, how you come across. This is what sets the interviewer's first and lasting impression of you.

2. Chemistry. That undefinable energy that ignites a relationship between two people will determine if you and the interviewer "hit it off."

3. Knowledge. You'll have to show what you know about the job, how you learned it, and how good you are.

4. Situation. The employer has certain constraints: a hiring time frame, job criteria that must be met, and salary limitations.

Employers often need to hire someone—NOW!

They Deal They want you! They're making job offer noises and gestures.

Now you're ready to negotiate your salary and benefits package. Always remember that everything is negotiable—though few people are trained or willing to negotiate for more!

How to Answer Questions That Ask You for Examples

Now that you're familiar with the general game plan interviewers use, let's get specific. It's time to take an in-depth look at what types of questions you're likely to be asked in an interview.

Many interviewers believe the best way to find out if people can really do what they claim is to ask them for concrete examples of job performance. Those able to readily volunteer detailed information usually score the most points with the interviewer.

Even though there are a number of different types of "example" questions, all good *answers* have some common elements. A good answer:

★ Presents the example in a logical fashion

★ Volunteers precise details about the situation

★ Shows that you are "results oriented"

• Three Steps to Developing Good Answers to Example Questions

There just are no standard answers for these questions—because everyone's life, educational, and work experiences are different. The best we can do is to introduce you to some typical questions, let you know what the interviewers are looking for, and show you three steps that you can take to come up with a solid answer. If you practice this three-step process, you'll be way ahead of the competition. To demonstrate the three steps, we'll start with a question about initiative on the job.

Question

Give me an example of when you've made a recommendation and it was accepted.

What the interviewer is looking for

★ Do you generate good ideas?

★ How did you demonstrate the value of the idea?

★ How hard do you push to get your ideas across?

Three Steps to Good Example Answers

Steps to Good Example Answers	*An Example Answer*
1. Choose your best example.	
2. Tell the story in detail.	
Where did this example take place? (Company name, department, city)	While I was working for Job Search Training Systems, in the book shipping department, in Nineveh, Indiana,
When did it take place? (The more recent the better.)	around June of 1994,
Why were you involved in this situation? (What problem were you trying to overcome?)	the order flow was screwed up. People weren't getting the shipments as quickly as they wanted.
Who else was involved? (Who were you working for during this situation? Who were you working with? Were you supervising anyone? Who else was involved in any way?)	At the time, there were five of us involved in shipping 20 to 30 orders per day. John Baker was our boss. I also had one person working under me and had to coordinate with the UPS driver.
What were you trying to achieve? (What results?)	We wanted to make sure that our orders were shipped the day after we received them.
How did you handle the situation? (What data, people skills, tools, or ideas did you use to deal with this situation?)	I wrote up my idea and presented the time-savings plan to my supervisor. I recommended that we dedicate one computer to order processing, change the forms, and rearrange pick-up time with the drivers.
3. Present the results.	
Did you reach your objective? How did you measure your success? How long did it take to achieve your goals? Talk numbers, quantify everything. Note: If the results weren't good, don't use them!	It must have worked. We used to get 10 to 20 late calls per week, now we're down to less than 5 and sometimes none. It took us only about three weeks to get all the bugs worked out and the system in place.

Now that you've seen how to apply the three-step process to developing a good "example answer," we'll consider a variety of different questions you may be asked. Don't just read them—instead, imagine that you are actually being asked each question. How would you answer? Practice answering, and in each case, remember to follow the three-step process: present your best example, describe the situation (tell the story), and indicate the results.

Questions on Initiative and Creativity

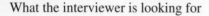

Question 1

Give me an example of when you've made a recommendation and it wasn't accepted.

What the interviewer is looking for

- ★ How you handle rejection
- ★ If you can learn from your mistakes
- ★ Will you use this new knowledge?

A sample answer

I presented what I thought was a good idea in a staff meeting. I wanted to develop a new brochure to market a product. What I didn't realize were the steps needed to get an idea like this implemented and how much the true cost was.

After I was "reamed" for not thinking the situation through, I asked a couple of the marketing folks to show me the steps they follow to actually come up with a new promo pack.

The next time I opened my mouth about a new idea, I can guarantee you that I knew what I was talking about. I've always heard it takes about a hundred ideas to get one up and running, and if you never try you never succeed.

Question 2

How much information do you need to get a project underway? Give an example of when you've been involved from the start.

What the interviewer is looking for

- ★ Are you self-motivated? Do you need a lot of information to get going?
- ★ How excited you are about accepting new challenges?

- ★ Levels of supervision needed to support you
- ★ Do you jump into something without thought?

A sample answer

I get excited about new projects and really like the whole process. In most instances I don't need a lot of "up front" time to get rolling. All I need to start is some basic direction from my supervisor: what they want, when they want it, how they want it. With this kind of information I'm at least not jumping in over my head—but I am getting the project moving forward.

At one of my former jobs (classes) . . .

Question 3

If you could change any one thing in your last job what would it be?

What the interviewer is looking for

- ★ Ability to assess situations
- ★ Well-thought-out, excited response
- ★ Does the suggestion make the job easier only for the employee, or does it make it easier for management too?

A sample answer

Being able to cut through some of the red tape would have been a big help. We could have been much more efficient handling paperwork. It was my opinion that too much time and staff effort was used to "shuffle" paper. If we could have reduced the number of people touching each piece of paper we'd have had more time to get other important tasks done.

Question 4

Describe a couple of innovations you're proud of.
(or)
Can you list any examples of your creativity?
(or)
What's the most creative thing you've done in your past jobs?

What the interviewer is looking for

- ★ Some idea of the supervision and training you'll need

★ If you *had* to be creative or if it's a natural part of you

★ Recent examples . . . the more recent the better

★ Did these examples have long-lasting effect?

A sample answer

One of the best examples of my creative or innovative capabilities would have to be the time I was requested to develop a company newsletter . . . all by myself. I'd never done anyting like this before but found it simpler than I thought. I reviewed a number of different newsletters from other companies and a few of the newsletters my husband receives. I also looked at the templates provided in Pagemaker software for newsletter development and set up a system for getting information from the other employees. We ended up with a newsletter format that's still being used by the company and that always gets compliments.

Question 5

Would you rather work a preplanned, routine day, or would you rather flow with the work schedule?

What the interviewer is looking for

★ Innovative people enjoy "playing it by ear"

★ Innovative people like "fluid" schedules

★ Innovators don't count hours, they count achievements

★ Someone who's not too flaky, disorganized, or lacking direction with their creative talents—be careful!

A sample answer

Even though I can and have worked well in a routine environment, if I could choose I'd prefer to flow with the work schedule. I seem to work pretty well in situations that utilize different skills and allow me to challenge myself . . . and see the results of my work. I've no problem with a flexible schedule or working overtime to get the job done.

Questions on Conflict Results

Work site conflicts negatively affect production and quality of work. They also wear on the nerves of management and workers both. There just isn't any place in today's labor market for such disruptions.

Question 1

Have you ever disagreed with a coworker? How did you handle the problem?

What the interviewer is looking for

★ Methods used to resolve problems

★ Whether you let your emotions affect your work

★ Your openness to other people's perspectives

★ Tact and willingness to compromise

★ Lasting effects on the situation

A sample answer

That just doesn't happen much. But I can remember one time when I didn't think one of my coworkers was pulling his weight.

At first I didn't say anything, hoping the problem would go away. When it didn't, I bought him some coffee and told him how his attitude was affecting me and my job performance. He said he had a few gripes himself, and we struck a "working deal."

It's been some time since we've had any real clash of wills. I think most work problems can be solved if you're willing to face them quickly.

Question 2

When your work is criticized, how do you react?

What the interviewer is looking for

★ How thick your skin is

★ Whether you get defensive instead of seeing the situation as an opportunity to learn

★ Whether the information goes in one ear and out the other

Sample answers

I'm not offended by much and have a pretty thick skin! (or)

I don't mind taking advice and guidance from anyone who can give it. (or)

Even though I've had my feelings hurt a couple of times, it's the price you have to pay if you want to have information laid out on the line.

Questions on Stress Management

Stress brings everyone to their knees sometime in life. It sort of goes with today's hectic world. If you can't find ways to overcome stress . . . you'll have more stress!

Question 1

How do you handle juggling multiple tasks and competing priorities?

What the interviewer is looking for

★ How you organize your tasks

★ Examples of resourcefulness

A sample answer

I can't remember a time when I've not juggled multiple duties—at work, in school, in my family life. The way I handle it is to create a prioritized "to do" list every morning and try to get rid of the tough stuff first. I've also learned the best way to avoid chaos is to not let it get started in the first place. For example . . .

Question 2

What situations put you under the most stress?

What the interviewer is looking for

★ Will stress potentially interfere with your work?

★ Is stress a continual or infrequent pressure?

★ Your reaction to high stress levels

A sample answer

I don't really find work situations all that stressful—most of the time. And I won't let my personal life interfere with my job. Even quotas and deadlines don't stress me out very much. There was one time when . . .

Questions on Decision Making

Decision-making skills are at the core of employment. Everyone who's ever been paid to work had to make decisions and sweated over them.

Question 1

How do you go about making decisions? Give an example of when you've had to make a decision quickly.

What the interviewer is looking for

★ Do you use logic, or do you rely on your feelings?

★ Do you pull other people in to help?

★ How do you gather information?

★ Do you take calculated risks?

A sample answer

One of my most difficult calls came when I was the senior customer service representative. One of our biggest customers demanded an immediate response to their request for a hefty refund . . . when my boss was on a two-week vacation. I used the decision making process I learned in our customer service classes. I defined the situation and compared it to our goals of customer satisfaction. I weighed the impact of losing this customer, caluclated the risk to myself and the company, identified the resources I'd need to make the choice and compared differ-ent alterneatives. Ultimately I decided to refund the money and take the heat. Two days later we received a letter from that customer saying they were increasing their yearly purchases because of this.

If decision making is a problem for you—as it is for a lot of people—or if you've never really thought about how you come to decisions, study our outline of a decision-making process (see sidebar). You can use it as the basis for your answer—it's okay to fudge a little!

The Decision-Making Process

Define the situation: How is the situation perceived as a problem, from different people's perspective? Why is it your responsibility to make a decision about it?

Define your goal: What do you hope to achieve with your decision? How will your decision affect other people and the company?

Identify resources and gather information: What do you need to know to make the choice? Who else is or needs to be involved?

Define parameters: How far will you go to achieve your objective? What calculated risks are you willing to take?

Project outcomes: Develop and compare different scenarios/options. Weigh each one against your goal and priorities.

Decide: Make up your mind. Also decide when and how you will follow up to see if the decision was a good one.

Questions on Organizational Skills

People able to manage projects can organize tasks, people, and data . . . and are considered better employees than those who can't.

Question 1

If you've ever planned a project from scratch, what steps did you take?

What the interviewer is looking for

★ Can you see the "big" picture, but also attend to detail?

★ Can you set goals and objectives and allocate resources?

★ Do you plan ahead and also follow through?

★ Can you delegate, supervise, and work with the team?

★ Do you enjoy this type of work?

A sample answer

I was responsible for developing an inventory tracking form and process. I followed a simple project management approach. I defined the objectives and tested them for reality, relevancy, and relatability. Once I figured out our objectives were sound I selected the best people for the job, defined each of their tasks, and set time frames for completion. I then determined performance standards and asked for help in evaluating alternative procedures. Based on this input, I had to alter completion time frames. As the project moved forward, I set up predetermined times to provide feedback. Once the project was completed I gave credit to those helping me, and, finally, set up a follow-up process to insure the forms worked well. Inventory losses were reduced 8–10 percent.

You may have never broken down and labeled the steps you have taken in managing a project—even if project management has been a substantial part of your work. We have outlined the steps that generally go into managing a project (see sidebar)—you can use it to formulate your answer: a little more fudging!

A Project Management Approach

1. Develop well-defined objectives. Test your objectives for
   • Reality (Can they be achieved?)
   • Relevancy (Are they important to the job?)
   • Relatability (Will other people get behind you?)
2. Select the most appropriate people to help.
3. Define the tasks. This includes setting time frames for completion and determining performance standards.
4. Seek out alternative opinions and ask for input.
5. Set predetermined times to give/get feedback.
6. "Talk up" the work done on the project and promote the value of the people helping you.
7. Set up a follow-up process to insure what you did is working well.

Questions on Goals and Ambitions

Career ambition questions are geared to finding out how much thought you've given to your future and how realistic you are about your career. People with realistic career expectations generally make the most happy employees. They tend to pose fewer problems and to be the employer's most productive workers.

Question 1

What are your future plans? Where do you see yourself in 18 months, 3 years, 5 years?

What the interviewer is looking for

★ Your understanding of the entire field, not just this job

★ Realistic, sequential, and attainable career objectives

★ Retainability. Will you stay after they train you?

★ Your willingness to do what's necessary to advance

A sample answer

I'm interested in developing a career, rather than just a job. My goal is to stay with a company and move from electronics technician to field representative—when I develop the skills to move up. I plan to do whatever's necessary to advance, including taking coursework that will improve my skills and value.

Question 2

What are your biggest achievements? Why did you select these?

What the interviewer is looking for

★ What motivates you and makes you proud of your work

★ Indicators of what you'll do to get things done

★ Indicators that you're likely to excel in the area

A sample answer

I liked the recognition I got when I won the Employee of the Week award for meeting all of my deadlines. Even though a couple of folks didn't show up that week, I worked through lunch and was still able to get all the reports collated and filed on time.

Prepare to have at least three achievements to talk about during the interview. Achievements can come from your life, work, and educational experience. Everybody has been successful at something. If you tell an interviewer you have no achievements, you're a fool—they'll believe you and pass you by.

Question 3

How would you describe an ideal day at work?

What the interviewer is looking for

★ What you talk about first is usually what you do best

★ What motivates you, time management, and use of the tools of the trade

A sample answer

I guess what I'd like to do most is take customer orders, enter the information into the computer, pack the orders, UPS them, and follow up with the customers to see if they're happy with their purchases.

I'd spend half my day doing this and the other half chasing down late payments. If I had time left, I'd look for something new to do.

A trick: An ideal work day can be described by reviewing a job description and regurgitating the information to the interviewer—in your own words.

Question 4

What do you want from this job, aside from a paycheck?

What the interviewer is looking for

★ Realistic expectations and desires in concrete terms

What Do You Want from This Job?

- Increased challenge
- Specific responsibilities and duties
- Ability to earn more money
- Better work environment (physical and/or emotional)
- Different kinds of people to work with
- A more secure field and company
- Higher levels of responsibility
- Enhanced job satisfaction
- Different working hours
- Less/more travel, overtime, etc.
- Ability to develop and use new skills
- Potential for career growth and advancement

A sample answer

Since most of my life will require that I work for a living, I want to make sure I end up in the right job. I've really given this question some thought.

If there's anything I really want from my next job, aside from a reasonable paycheck, it's the ability to learn new skills, have better advancement opportunity, and be given more responsibility for my own time and performance.

Question 5

Why did you apply at this company?

Those who research and "select" a company for which to work usually have higher levels of attendance, seem to manage their time more effectively, and are more profitable employees—probably because they've carefully considered where they want to work and are happy to be there. When an interviewer asks you this question, you need to demonstrate that you researched the company and chose to apply for good reasons.

What the interviewer is looking for

★ Indicators of planning and organization skills

★ Predictors of analytical thinking and decision making

• How Did You Find Out about the Company?

1. You have a personal knowledge of company's products or services.
2. You did library research on the company.
3. You talked to people working at the company.
4. You've been inside and seen how things worked.
5. You read/heard/saw a company advertisement.
6. You sent for company literature.
7. An acquaintance recommended the company.
8. You've had business dealings with the company.
9. You've worked for/researched the competition.
10. You called and asked questions.

• What Did You Find Out about the Company?

1. You know the company uses people with your skills, abilities, and educational background.
2. The company has a good community reputation.
3. They're seen as leaders in the field.
4. The company has good growth potential.
5. You can get job satisfaction at this company.
6. Geographically, it's where you want to be.
7. The company rewards people based on merit.
8. The company provides a valuable service/product.
9. The company has a good reputation for advancement.
10. The personality of the company matches your own.

Choose from these two lists and you'll have all the information you need to answer this question.

Questions on Personal Motivation

Personal motivation is a big topic for interviewers. People excited about themselves and how they interact with their job are perceived as leaders, shakers, and doers. People who make rational career choices, for specific reasons, are seen as self-motivated and are what every employer is looking for in today's labor market. Be one!

Question 1

Why did you choose this particular line of work?

What the interviewer is looking for

★ Well-defined reasons for your career choice

★ How excited you are about working in the field

★ They *don't* want to hear that you "lucked into it."

A sample answer

I've always had an interest in working with disabled people. I grew up with a disabled younger brother and know that my personality fits this kind of work.

Aside from my first-hand experience, I did some library research on occupational therapy, took a few career tests, and talked with folks in the field, before I began taking college courses.

Question 2

What motivates you to do exceptional work?

What the interviewer is looking for

★ To match your motivations against what the job demands.

Select Your Top 10 Motivators (And You Have the Makings of a Good Answer)

- The opportunity to help society and others improve their life
- Frequent public contact
- Working with others as part of a team
- To be able to compete for salary and advancement
- To make independent decisions about doing the job
- Power and authority
- Control over day-to-day situations
- To gain knowledge, research information
- To be exposed to new ideas
- To be creative and innovative
- A quick-paced environment
- To be recognized (financially) for a job well done
- Some level of excitement in my day
- To show my physical abilities or attributes
- Use my special knowledge and talents
- To bring home "big bucks"
- Control over my time and responsibility
- Moral fulfillment
- Involvement with community affairs
- To develop and expand my talents
- To have a prestigious job title
- To be able to express my opinions at work
- To be challenged in my work
- Personal enjoyment from the job
- To take risks as part of the job
- To be in the public eye
- To use my problem-solving ability
- To immediately see the results of my efforts
- To be seen as a leader in my field

Common Reasons for Choosing a Career

- You talked with people working in the field and became interested.
- Your educational interests match the field.
- Aptitude tests indicate you'd be good at the job.
- Career counseling led you into the field.
- You've done an in-depth self-assessment.
- Something about the field excites you. (What?)
- You've explored the field. It matches your goals.
- You have related work experiences.
- Your skills and abilities match the job demands.
- You've got a personality that fits the job.
- You've always had an interest in the field.

Hot Questions

Hot questions are general questions about *you*. The interviewer wants to see what you think of yourself! Feel free to blow your own horn, but keep it short and always relate what you're saying to how well you could do the job.

Most job seekers really blow this first question by focusing on their desire for the job, rather than on the employer's concern.

Question 1

Why should I hire you?

What the interviewer is looking for

★ People who can get along

★ People who won't present problems

★ People willing to do more work—employers are interested in profit!

Tell the interviewer you've given this a lot of thought. Select five of the following reasons and build yourself a knock-your-socks-off interview answer.

Why an Employer Would Be Happy to Hire Me

- I'm interested in helping you make more profit.
- I'm willing to work hard and be productive.
- I'm quality-oriented.
- I can get along with supervisors and coworkers.
- I know how to increase the company's visibility.
- I have a solid history of being reliable.
- My attendance record is better than average.
- My record of punctuality is better than average.
- I'm more than willing to work overtime.
- I have a proven success record.
- My transferable skills complement the job demands.
- My personality fits the job.
- I have a long-term interest in this field.
- My education has prepared me for the job.
- I try to learn new things all the time.
- I'm interested in a career—not just a job.
- I have a personal drive to do good work.
- I can bring my leadership skills to the job.
- My energy level is higher than most people's.
- I'm willing to take on responsibility.
- I feel like I owe a day's work for a day's pay.
- I won't ask for raises until I'm due them.
- I can work with minimal supervision.
- I have the potential to move up.
- I've researched the job and company and know this is what I want.
- Tests show I have the aptitude for this job.
- I have a good moral character.
- I'm loyal to companies willing to invest in me.
- I'm willing to accept instructions from others.
- I'm willing to give people help.
- My honesty has never been questioned.
- I'll do extra work in order to get ahead.
- You can count on me when times are tough.

Question 2

What do you consider to be your greatest strengths?

Many people have trouble with this question since it seems like they're tooting their own horn—but if you don't no one else will. Always remember this about bragging: If you can back it up, it's not bragging—it's fact! Always have at least three strengths for presentation.

What the interviewer is looking for

★ a skills match of your strengths to their needs

★ provable examples rather than unsubstantiated statements

★ achievements and successes

★ what you'll bring to the company that others don't

The following list gives you some acceptable strengths to choose from if you're having trouble defining your own. If you can't back them up with examples, don't choose them.

1. I am on time for the job and I complete my work on time.

2. I try to have a near perfect attendance record.

3. I'm willing to work overtime, weekends, and holidays.

4. I do good work.

5. I ask questions.

6. I'm honest with the company's time and materials.

7. I have good communication and interpersonal skills.

8. I can give instructions to people needing help.

9. I'm willing to accept instruction from others.

10. I'm reliable. Count on me to get things done.

11. I follow rules and company procedures.

12. I look for ways to work smarter.

13. I'm always looking for ways to save money.

14. I have good listening skills.

15. I enjoy working.

16. My work production is higher than the average.

17. I'm loyal and dedicated to my employer.

18. I don't expect to get ahead unless I do extra work.

19. I'm a problem solver: I try to think things through.

20. I learn new things quickly.

21. I can work with minimal supervision.

A sample answer

Since most of my working life has been spent in a small manufacturing company, I'd have to say that my best strengths are my interpersonal skills, my production capabilities, and my interest in learning more efficient ways to get the job done. In my last job I met every production quota, never had any real problems interacting with my co-workers, supervisors, or management, and I was one of the few people in the plant who could always be relied on to take every seminar offered that kept my job skills up to date.

Question 3

What is your major weakness?

This question strikes fear in the hearts of many job seekers. It's important to avoid responses that present negative information on the one hand, or indicate that you are a "perfect" worker on the other. The best approach is to talk about an area you're working on improving.

What the interviewer is looking for

★ They're looking for you to volunteer negative information!

A sample answer

Avoid the word "weakness"	*I don't know that I want to call it a weakness,*
State improvement area	*but I've been working on improving my computer skills.*
State why important	*I found computer graphics skills useful in my last job*
Show how you are improving	*so I began taking courses and buying books.*
Show how this helps	*I think this shows that I can spot areas for improvement and then act on them.*

Question 4

Can you tell me a little bit about yourself?

This question is considered the granddaddy of all interview questions. If you don't handle this one well, you may not get the chance to handle many others. A good answer would indicate that you have given this question a lot of thought since you knew you'd only have a few minutes to respond during the interview. A good answer would also briefly cover the following topics: your job objective, your education and experience, your skills, your achievements, and your motivation or dedication.

THOU SHALT

practice answering this question

...over and over and over and over and over and over and over

A sample answer

State job objective	*I'm interested in a career in warehouse operations.*
State experience	*I have over three years experience from my past work and educational experiences*
Create "skills linkage"	*where I did similar work and used related skills.*
Stress job skills	*I'm able to operate all materials-handling equipment and to perform shipping, receiving, and order-filling functions. I can also do inventory control and scheduling.*
Talk about education	*I've taken courses in school and in the military. I've also taken on-the-job training seminars.*
Hit transferable skills	*I can train people, am safety conscious, and consider myself well organized.*
Tag fitting-in skills	*I work hard, I'm reliable, and I get along with my coworkers, customers, and supervisors.*
Indicate dedication	*I'm the kind of person who's loyal to an employer, and I can always be counted on.*
Cite success	*One of my biggest points of pride was coming up with an idea about how to reduce accidents. Injuries dropped 10 percent when we implemented my plan.*
Return the question	*I hope this gives you an overview of what I can bring to the company. What else would you like to know that I haven't brought up?*

Dependability, Flexibility, and Cooperation Questions

It can cost employers anywhere from about $600 to a full year's salary to recruit, select, train . . . and then lose an employee. People who move from one job to another without good cause are usually considered less eligible for hire than those who have a sound rationale for job changing.

---

10 Acceptable Reasons for Hitting the Bricks

Security	Advancement
Family	Money
Challenge	Change in management
Satisfaction	Reduction in force
Location	Professional pride

Question 1

Why do you want to leave your present job?

What the interviewer is looking for

★ Someone who's retainable and trainable—and won't pack their trash and leave at the drop of a hat!

★ Rational, well-thought-out reasons for the change

A sample answer

This was a tough choice. I liked my previous job but wanted more challenge, more responsibility, and the opportunity to learn to use more sophisticated equipment. There just weren't those types of opportunities at my last job.

It happens—even to the best of workers—for a number of reasons. One 1993 survey by AccounTemps says 33 percent of all employees will probably be fired sometime, and 80 percent of employers don't think firing carries the stigma it did a few years back.

Question 2

Why were you fired?

What the interviewer is looking for

- ★ Honesty
- ★ Your willingness to take responsibility for your actions
- ★ Indicators that you have learned from your experience

A sample answer

Be honest	*I want to be honest, I was let go from my job.*
Show remorse	*I'm sorry I screwed up,*
Be responsible	*I deserved what I got.*
Explain (briefly)	*I didn't show up for work during a time when things needed to be done and it adversely affected the other people in the department.*
Learn from error	*This has taught me a lesson that I won't soon forget.*
Make commitment	*I don't know what else to say other than I won't let you down.*
Relate	*Have you ever done something you wish you could redo or take back?*

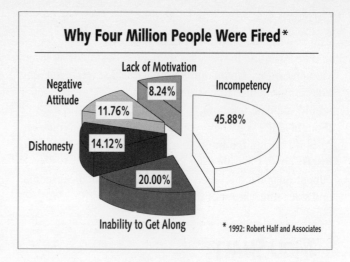

Why Four Million People Were Fired*

- Lack of Motivation 8.24%
- Negative Attitude 11.76%
- Incompetency 45.88%
- Dishonesty 14.12%
- Inability to Get Along 20.00%

* 1992: Robert Half and Associates

A trick: Let the interviewer know you understand why people get fired and share the information from the chart on this page.

Job hoppers cost employers bundles of bucks each year. It takes time, money, and energy to recruit, train, develop, and . . . lose workers.

Question 3

Why have you held so many jobs?

What the interviewer is looking for

- ★ An understandable reason for continual change
- ★ Indicators that you won't be with them long

Some Reasons for Making a Move

1. You're always looking for more job satisfaction.
2. Your immaturity and youth overrode your common sense.
3. You just needed survival jobs at that time in your life.
4. You had to take care of family needs or other personal commitments instead of focusing on your career goals at that time in your life.
5. You wanted to experiment in different fields/jobs before settling on a career.
6. You wanted to spend time traveling while you were still young.
7. It was part of your personality and you used to be willing to pay the price for it.
8. Your lifestyle (or that of your parents, if applicable) wasn't conducive to long-term work.

9. Your former occupations (example: migrant worker, etc.) weren't conducive to continuous employment.

10. You've made a lot of mistakes which forced you into and out of employment.

11. You wrongly felt the grass was greener somewhere else . . . more than just once!

If you choose any of the responses that might be considered negative reasons—1, 4, 7, 8, 10, 11—you must be ready to convince the interviewer that you're a changed person by telling him or her how and why you have since changed your situation, behavior, or mind-set—what makes you a good risk now?

Job gaps

in today's topsy-turvy world of layoffs aren't considered uncommon. Twenty percent of America's workers will be unemployed sometime during the year.

Question 4

Why have you been unemployed so long?

What the interviewer is looking for

★ An understandable reason for your unemployment

★ How you spent this period of time

Acceptable Reasons for Extended Unemployment

1. Waited too long to be called back from layoff

2. The economy took a downturn in your line of work

3. Couldn't find work which best used your skills

4. Had to stay in a certain location

5. Made a commitment that took priority over work

6. Decided to finish or continue your education

7. Took time to research the type of work you wanted

8. Took time to get job counseling

9. Didn't need to work at that time

10. Stayed home to raise a family

11. Stayed home to take care of family members

12. You and your spouse split house/work duties

13. Took a vacation before re-entering job market

14. Wanted to do volunteer work

15. Spouse didn't want you to work at that time

Acceptable Ways to Spend Time While Unemployed

Aside from defining your reason for the job gap, interviewers often want to know what you did during that period of time. Were you doing things that would help improve your value as an applicant? Or did you spend your time on more personal issues: health, family care, etc. If you fall into this latter category you may want to talk to a job search professional or a rehabilitation counselor. Be prepared to talk about why you decided to invest your time this way, focus on how the time spent will make you a better candidate/worker, and stress that these issues are no longer an employment concern.

★ Improving job knowledge through school, skills training, seminars

★ Improving self-knowledge through counseling, self-assessment, self-help books

★ Selecting your best career through testing, research, experimentation

★ Taking care of yourself through therapy, thinking time, hospitalization

★ Taking care of personal matters, such as home repair, time with kids, time with spouse

★ Trading room and board for work

Questions on Job Performance and Accomplishments

If you can't define what's needed for success, the chances are the employer will believe you don't have it.

Question 1

What do you think is needed to be successful in this type of work?

What the interviewer is looking for

- ★ Your job skills
- ★ Other transferable skills and personality traits

A sample answer

Aside from my job skills [list up to 10 of your most powerful job skills—see page 8], *which are required to do a quality job, I think a good worker...* [Remember as many of the following as you can and you'll have a great answer.]

- ★ shows initiative
- ★ can handle stress
- ★ is self-motivated
- ★ has good attendance
- ★ is punctual
- ★ exhibits creativity
- ★ is innovative
- ★ can solve problems
- ★ has career ambitions
- ★ can learn quickly
- ★ is dependable
- ★ is flexible
- ★ has organizational skills

- ★ can manage his/her own time
- ★ pays attention to detail
- ★ uses interpersonal skills
- ★ handles conflict well
- ★ is cooperative

Question 2

What did you dislike most about your previous employment?

The Rule of Proof

If you say you did it, you must always be able to give three examples.

What the interviewer is looking for

- ★ If you'll "bad-mouth" your former employers!
- ★ Possible performance and personality problem areas

A sample answer

Although there are always tough days on any job, I'd really have to say that I didn't "hate" anything. There were some things I liked about the job more than others, but that never held me back from doing good work.

At my last job, I liked operating the computers and using spreadsheet programs. I also had a lot of fun talking with customers and solving their problems.

Never Ever Rule

Question 3

What would you say is your biggest accomplishment?

What the interviewer is looking for

★ Indicators of skills and problem-solving abilities

★ Indicators of innovative thinking

To answer this question well, think seriously about when you

★ Surpassed yourself in job performance

★ Made something simpler or got it done quicker or with fewer resources

★ Developed something new, from scratch

All Accomplishments Are Measurable

- Improved quality
- Increased sales
- Reduced costs
- Increased profits
- Improved employee relations
- Improved productivity
- Developed working teams
- Reduced times
- Achieved technological process
- Established administrative process
- Planned program from scratch

Effort's commendable—but only results count!

A sample answer

I was working for a very small educational software development company. We wanted to develop an instructional package that was capable of beating the competition's, but we really didn't have the kind of money or resources they had and we weren't able to utilize their proprietary application programs. So I led a team of two other software engineers and developed a new application, from scratch and in a relatively short period of time, that surpassed the competition's. We made our development process simpler and increased our profits by reducing the overall development costs—and now we had our own proprietary application.

Questions on Fitting-in Skills

Questions about interpersonal issues give the interviewer clues about your fitting-in skills—and poor answers can kill your job opportunities in a heartbeat.

Many of these types of questions are *situations*, and no one can give you a "pat" answer. But we know what concerns the interviewer, and you can develop answers based on that.

Interview Success Rule #4

Always Stress Teamwork and Dedication

Question 1

Give an example of when you've disagreed with someone on the job. How did you handle it?

What the interviewer is looking for

★ Assertive people unafraid to constructively disagree

An acceptable answer should answer the following:

★ Who was involved, and what was their relationship to you?

★ What was the problem you wanted to overcome?

★ What did you do to overcome it?

★ What were the positive results of your approach?

A sample answer

One instance I remember vividly was when a co-worker and I had to team up on a sales presentation project and we disagreed on the best way to construct it. I wanted to use a lot of graphics, she wanted to put it into a written proposal format. Neither of us had authority over the other but we had equal responsibility for getting the job done. After some bickering we decided to develop three lists: the pros and cons of each approach; the time and costs of the different approaches; and the issues we felt we were in agreement on. We found our differing approaches had more in common than we thought and we ended up combining both methods—and getting the sale.

Question 2

How would you describe your personality?

What the interviewer is looking for

★ Fitting-in skills and personality traits that match the job

For the best answer, look at your list of fitting-in skills on the job offer generator grid on page 21. Use those words with a support statement. Here's a sample.

Fitting-in Skill	Support Statement
I'm loyal.	I'm committed to my employer.
I'm dedicated.	I want a long-term job relationship.
I'm a team player.	I learned there was no "I" in team.

Question 3

What will your references say about you?
(or)
Would your former employers hire you again?

What the interviewer is looking for

★ Risk reduction: past experiences = future experiences

Reference checking is one of the top four methods employers use to determine if an applicant is likely to work out on the job. You can't afford to leave your references to chance.

Make a list of former supervisors, coworkers, and subordinates you would consider asking for references. Ask yourself how each would evaluate you (excellent, good, fair, rotten) on the reference-checking items below. (Photocopy this list, and fill out one for each reference.) Select your top 10, let your references know what you're going to say, and ask them to confirm these traits when called.

Interview Success Rule #5

Always research the company literature and call for information before an interview.

_____ Punctuality

_____ Attendance

_____ Willingness to work overtime

_____ Willingness to do the job until it's done right

_____ Honesty with company time and materials

_____ Technical knowledge

_____ Interpersonal skills

_____ Oral communication

_____ Respect for supervisor(s)

_____ Ability to instruct others

_____ Ability to accept instructions

_____ Writing skills

_____ Relevant math skills

_____ Moral character

_____ Work quality

_____ Work quantity

_____ Company loyalty

_____ Willingness to do extra work to get ahead

_____ History of success

_____ Future potential

_____ Ability to learn

_____ Ability to work with minimal supervision

_____ Leadership skills

_____ Managing, delegating, motivating skills

_____ Decision making and planning

_____ Analytical abilities

_____ Conceptual skills

_____ Adaptability

_____ Time management skills

_____ Stress management

_____ Ability to cope with deadlines

Question 4

What have you learned from your previous managers that would help you on this job?

What the interviewer is looking for

- ★ Type of management under which you work the best

- ★ Level of cooperation and support you give

- ★ Respect for and understanding of authority

A good answer should describe two or three things you've learned from people you've worked under and how they got this information across to you. You should also explain how the things you learned helped you to be a better worker. Your answer should *never* include any harsh statements about your managers.

A sample answer

I guess I'd have to say I learned quite a bit from all the people I've worked for—and with, for that matter. But the most important thing I think I've learned from watching all of my managers is the importance of handling multiple tasks. If you can't juggle more than one thing at a time, you just can't be as productive and you stress out quicker.

**The #1 Trait of All Managers
is the Ability to Get People
to Work Together
Toward a Common Goal!**

Question 5

How would you describe a good manager?

What the interviewer is looking for

- ★ An understanding of the traits needed to be successful

- ★ Indicators of possible conflicts with the person who would be your boss

- ★ Possibilities for adding responsibilities to your job

- ★ Those areas in which you'll probably be the most effective

A sample answer

Superior managers have a vision of where they're going and are able to excite their workers with that vision. They are excellent role models because of their good judgment and their decision-making skill. They are comfortable exercising authority and delegating tasks. And above all, they are able to get people to work together.

Question 6

Have you ever disagreed with one of your supervisor's decisions? What did you do?

What the interviewer is looking for

- ★ Ability to disagree in a healthy way

- ★ Passive and active resistance patterns

- ★ Whether you got on board once the decision was made

A good answer would show your understanding of why and how the decision was made and ways you've made the best of the situation. There should be no blame or indication that you stayed mad.

A sample answer

Yes, I'd have to say I disagreed when someone else got the promotion I wanted!

There were a few of us bidding for the job, and we all had about the same experience. I don't want to say I was mad that someone else was promoted, but I wasn't happy either.

When I talked to my boss, she indicated the reasons for the choice. I still didn't agree . . . but that's water under the bridge. I found out what I needed to get considered next time and I've been working on those areas ever since.

Question 7

What type of people do you like the most and get along with the best?

What the interviewer is looking for

★ An appreciation of close working relationships

★ A personality match to existing workers and the workplace's interpersonal environment

A sample answer

I'd much rather develop good relationships with my coworkers than to just stay in my little corner of the company. If the coworkers don't like each other, the work life can get a little tough.

The people I spend the most time with are sort of fun-loving, they're loyal, they really like their work, and are family-oriented. I guess likes do attract.

At my last job we had to compete against other departments—I think these contests helped us get along better.

Questions on Education

Questions concerning your educational experience give interviewers clues about your early achievements, special knowledge, and commitment level. They also want to see if your education is relevant to the job at hand and whether you've pursued education in order to advance your career.

Question 1

How has your education prepared you for the job?

What the interviewer is looking for

★ What you know

★ Where you learned it

★ How well you learned it

★ How it will help the employer

After you fill in the information on this page and the next, you should be well prepared to answer most questions that come your way on this topic.

List any course work you've taken that would be relevant to the type of work you're seeking.

College/University programs

_____
_____
_____
_____
_____

On-the-job training (OJT)

_____
_____
_____
_____

Seminars

_____
_____
_____
_____

Correspondence courses

_____
_____
_____
_____

Independent study

_____
_____
_____
_____

What interpersonal skills did you develop in school?

_____
_____
_____
_____
_____

What data skills did you learn in school?

_____

_____

_____

_____

What tools/machines/equipment did you learn to operate?

_____

_____

_____

_____

What are your biggest educational achievements?

_____

_____

_____

_____

Question 2

If you didn't complete your education, why?

What the interviewer is looking for

★ Non-completion patterns

★ Training problems

A good answer would explain your reason for quitting and what you're doing to complete your education now. You should emphasize other commitments that you *have* kept or tasks you've successfully completed. State your long-range education and career goals too.

Questions on Learning Ability and Problem Solving

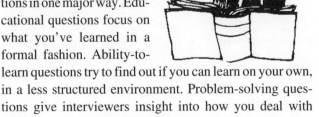

Ability-to-learn questions differ from educational questions in one major way. Educational questions focus on what you've learned in a formal fashion. Ability-to-learn questions try to find out if you can learn on your own, in a less structured environment. Problem-solving questions give interviewers insight into how you deal with adverse and unexpected situations. Always remember, "A job is nothing more than solving problems." The applicant who shows he or she can handle more problems is often considered the best candidate for the job.

Question 1

If there's one thing you'd like to learn, or skill you'd like to develop, what would it be?

What the interviewer is looking for

★ Whether you can assess your own skills and deficiencies

★ If you're motivated to learn new things

★ Whether what you want to learn will enhance your value to the employer

A sample answer

One thing I'd like to learn to do is how to use graphics on the computer. I know the future is heading toward multimedia, and if I want to keep up I'm going to have to pick these skills up myself.

If the company's willing to help me learn, I'm more than willing to invest the effort. And if I learned well enough, I'd be able to teach other people.

Question 2

What's the quickest you've ever learned something new on the job?

What the interviewer is looking for

★ Indicators of your ability to learn quickly

★ How you learn new skills and duties most effectively

A sample answer

In one of my previous jobs, I had to learn to use a word processor and spreadsheet package in less than a week. I took evening training courses during that week, so I'd still be able to keep up with my other duties, and used what I learned each evening in the following day's work.

Initially I was sort of embarrassed about attending the classes. I thought I'd be way behind everyone else. What I found was that I could pick up practical skills in a pretty short period.

Many employers believe that if you can handle the problem of job hunting in an efficient manner, the odds are you'll be able to take on others just as well. From our perspective this is a solid indicator of a person's potential.

Question 3

How are you currently looking for work?

What the interviewer is looking for

- ★ Whether you defined your goals and objectives
- ★ What level of effort you are making
- ★ Research and analytical skills
- ★ Risk-taking and motivational traits

This is the easiest question of them all . . . if you're following our lead. Just tell the employer

- ★ What you want
- ★ What you've done so far
- ★ What you're doing now

Question 4

What's the most difficult problem you've had to overcome or the most difficult decision you've had to make (aside from looking for work)?

What the interviewer is looking for

- ★ Your approach to problems—do you see problems as disasters or as challenges?
- ★ How you overcame the situation—what specific skills and traits came into play?

A good answer could address what happens if you don't deal with problem situations. It would include a specific example of a problem or decision you faced, why it was important, and how you dealt with it.

A sample answer

I had to decide whether or not to put my father in a nursing home. Even though we both knew I couldn't care for his medical needs, he didn't want to go. I tried a number of alternatives, but nothing worked out. Ultimately logic had to overcome emotion.

Question 5

What's your biggest mistake?

Watch out! Don't use an example from work if possible.

Your answer should touch on your willingness to take responsibility for your actions and should explain where you went wrong and what you did to rectify the situation.

A sample answer

Although I've made more than one of them, my biggest would probably be the time I chose to go on vacation to Hawaii with my wife. I got cheap after looking at the cost. I found a "deal" on airfare and lodging—if we went during a certain time of the year, stayed at a certain group of hotels, and were willing to pay some money up front. We ended up spending tons of time in the airport waiting for "space available" flights and staying in sleazy motels during the rainy season. We paid more than we would have had I used the travel agent I talked to in the first place. Never again!

Questions on Attendance and Time Management

There's one overriding employment principle: If you're not there to do the work, the work won't get done!

Question 1

What obstacles have you had to overcome to get to work on time?

Who Misses the Most Work

Type of Business	Days Absent
Agricultural wage and salary workers	3.8
Finance, insurance, and real estate	3.8
Wholesale and retail	4.3
Transportation and public utilities	4.5
Manufacturing	4.6
Mining	4.7
Private nonagricultural wage and salary workers	4.7
Construction	5.0
Services	5.2
Government workers	5.5

What the interviewer is looking for

★ Whether you can be counted on

★ How you manage your time

The best way to answer is to talk "worst-case" scenarios: your toilet overflowed, but you still made it in. Describe how you've handled child care, school schedules, traffic problems, emergency situations, etc.

Question 2

What do you think is an acceptable attendance rate?

What the interviewer is looking for

★ Two words: work ethic!

A sample answer

I just read in the Almanac that most people miss about five days per year. That's somewhere close to a 98 percent attendance rate. That sounds about right to me.

Question 3

Will you be available for weekend and overtime work?

Unless serious religious or family issues take precedent, there's only one answer. . .

Question 4

If you've missed more than a few days of work, why?

What the interviewer is looking for

★ Chronic or severe illness

★ Conflicts between home and work life

A good answer would include a brief story about what caused you to take off. Stress the fact that you always make up any work. Indicate that the situation is no longer a factor, or rarely arises.

Question 5

Can you give an example of when you've had to meet deadlines?

What the interviewer is looking for

★ How you respond to pressure

★ If you give extra effort to get a job done on time

It's important to answer with at least one concrete example, including names and titles of the people involved. Describe the time constraints you were under, the ramifications of not meeting the deadline, what actions you took to get the work done, and at least one positive result from your efforts.

Question 6

What do you do if you get bored on the job?

What the interviewer is looking for

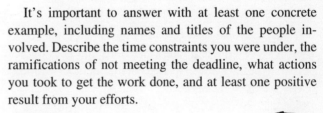

★ Whether you use time constructively

★ How much supervision you may require

★ Indicators of growth potential

★ Predictors of your teamwork skills

A sample answer

I'm usually working enough not to get bored. But on those few occasions when that's happened, I look for something new to do or learn, take care of paperwork, or help someone else out.

At my last job I used my free time to learn the bookkeeping software when the bookkeeper needed some help.

Questions on Money

The big trick to negotiating for a higher salary is timing! Once they say they want you, you're worth more.

So always try to get the interviewer to commit to hiring you *before* you talk money and benefits.

And know your worth. Call your local job service office or chamber of commerce before your interview for your area's prevailing wage.

Question 1

How much do you expect to be paid?

A sample answer

When the interviewer asks you any money questions, first ask:

Is this a job offer?

If not, then say:

Why don't we talk money and benefits after we define the job's duties and responsibilities and decide whether or not we'll be working together?

If the interviewer says, "Our range is . . .," bracket it. In other words, quote a range that starts and ends higher than what the interviewer quoted but that includes a middle ground where you can meet.

Bracketing

Employer says the salary range is...
$25,000 to $30,000
You say your range is...
$28,000 to $33,000

Both of You Are Winners!

Salary Negotiation Rule #1

Everything is Negotiable!

Salary Negotiation Rule #2

Employers Don't Get Upset with People Who Negotiate!

If you really need the job and the salary is below what you need to make, try this approach:

I'm more than willing to start out at this rate to prove my value, but what would I have to do to earn $___, and how long would it take me to get to that point?

Questions to Ask the Interviewer

Although it may sometimes seem like it, having an interview is not simply a question of submitting to a "firing squad" of interviewer questions. It's not a one-way street—*you* get to ask questions too! In fact, it's your best chance to interview the employer, to see if the job meets your criteria.

Those who ask the best questions will get the most useful answers, will survive the "interview test" the best, and will be remembered the longest. Well-thought-out questions show the interviewer you're bending over backward to be sure you're a good match to the job, the company, the supervisor, and the coworkers—and can really set you apart from the competition.

? Asking Questions Rule #1 ?

Ask questions that say something about your ability to fit in, do the job, and meet the company objectives.

? Asking Questions Rule #2 ?

Hold off asking about benefits until you get an offer. Then you'll be in control!

Each of the following questions are ones employers like to hear. They focus on teamwork, loyalty and dedication, and career growth. And they give the interviewer a better picture of how you'll fit in with the company.

★ What specific job duties and responsibilities are the most important to getting the job done as part of the team?

★ How do you like to operate in terms of delegation of authority, responsibility, and assignments?

★ What characteristics do you like most and least in a subordinate? (Yes, this is a kiss-up question—but a good one for getting critical information. Give a little, get a little!)

★ What criteria would be used to evaluate my performance, and how often would I be appraised?

★ What's the normal path and time frame for advancement within the company?

★ What are the major areas of accountability for this position?

★ Is the position sharply defined, or can it be expanded and changed?

★ How have other people handled this position? What did they do well, and where did they screw up?

★ What's the biggest problem you've had with the people who've held this job before?

★ What could I expect to face in the first month, three months, six months on the job?

★ What would you like me to achieve in three, six, nine, twelve months?

★ How much authority and responsibility would I have?

★ To whom would I be most directly responsible?

★ With whom would I be most closely working and what are their responsibilities?

★ If I'm filling a job opening, why did my predecessor leave?

★ What is the mission statement of the company/ division/department that I would join?

★ Do you have a job description available? (You should already have one of these before the interview; if not, get one now.)

★ When will you be making a decision, and what's the process?

 Asking Questions Rule #3

Don't just use our questions—even though they are pretty good. Think for yourself and develop a series of questions you think would help you learn more—and impress the interviewer!

How to Close the Interview and Follow Up

WE'LL CALL YOU!

"Don't call us—we'll call you!" How many job seekers have heard some version of this line at the end of the interview? It's so standard it's a joke.

The end of the interview is a critical time—the time to reinforce the interviewer's (hopefully) good impression of you. But many job seekers really miss the boat at this time. In fact, fewer than 5 percent make the extra effort to implant themselves in the interviewer's memory.

But you can be one of that small percentage. Here are seven easy steps that will help you leave a positive lasting impression.

• 7 Steps for a Lasting Impression

1. Thank interviewer by name

2. Express interest in the job and the company

3. Verbally reinforce that you can and will do the job

4. Request opportunity to follow up

5. Write down call-back date and time

6. Restate thank you

7. Leave one or more skills summary cards

When they say, "We'll call you," you say:

1. Thanks for taking the time with me, Mrs. Shagnasty.

2. I'm really interested in the job and working for the company.

3. I'm sure I have the skills to do quality work and I promise you I won't let you/the company down.

4. I would appreciate the chance to get back with you to follow up and to answer any questions you might still have and the ones I'm sure I'll come up with—as soon as I leave!

5. When's the best time for me to do this? [Get a specific time and date and make a note of it.]

6. Again, I'd like to thank you for your time, and I'll be calling [date and time].

7. [As you leave give the interviewer one or more of your skills summary cards.] Oh! Here's a summary of my skills—just so you don't forget me.

• Don't Forget to Say Thank You!

Always follow up your interview with a thank-you note—immediately. Why? First of all, it's a common courtesy. Thank-you notes aren't received as often as you might think and employers appreciate them. Also, they give you a chance to reinforce your skills and to counter any mistakes you might have made during the interview. Most employers like to see this kind of persistence.

Besides, a thank-you note shows a little class!

What Goes into a Thank-you Note?

- Your personal thanks
- Expressions of excitement about the job
- Brief review of your skills
- A promise you'd do good work

A Sample KISS Thank-you Note

Dear Mr. Teague,

Thank you for your time and for the information you gave me about your company during the interview.

I'm really excited about the position we discussed, and I'm sure my business and machine operation skills can contribute to the company.

Since my background includes successful experience in quality control management, I know I can be a big help with your new manufacturing process.

Again, my thanks for your consideration. I'm looking forward to becoming one of your more dedicated workers and team members.

Sincerely,

Les Johnson

Les Johnson

The Quest for Job Leads

Your Personal Referral Network

Quick review time! If you've done your work, you now have the mindset, the job search tools, and the basic interviewing skills to find the labor market—and effectively attack it.

So where is the job market hiding? It's not! How can it be? There's always job growth—somewhere. We know there are about 120 million people who are currently in the labor force. The job market revealed itself to *them*. What did they do?

• The Two Best Ways to Find Leads

The two best search methods are:

1. Directly contacting the hiring authority, either face to face or by phone.

2. Using your referral network of friends, relatives, neighbors, and acquaintances.

Chapter 5 covers the first method in detail, so now we'll concentrate on networking.

The 1st Rule of Networking

Everyone knows someone...who knows someone else... who knows someone else...who knows...

Interview Network Formula

20–40 interviews = 200–400 network contacts

The Ultimate Rule of Networking

It is who you know that counts!

• Your Network Database

Nobody really remembers everyone they know . . . until Christmas, or when they come back from vacation with too few gifts. This list is designed to jog your memory so you can expand your referral network. Your job is to create a database of who you know.

Personal contacts

* ★ Friends
* ★ Neighbors
* ★ Relatives
* ★ Creditors
* ★ Social club members
* ★ Fraternity/sorority brothers/sisters
* ★ Athletic teammates
* ★ Former classmates
* ★ Convention participants

Work contacts

* ★ Coworkers
* ★ Vendors
* ★ Subcontractors
* ★ Customers
* ★ Competitors
* ★ Travel contacts

Acquaintances

* ★ Political contacts
* ★ Religious contacts
* ★ Teachers
* ★ Placement staff

* ★ Grocers
* ★ Barbers, hairdressers
* ★ Mechanics
* ★ Fund raisers
* ★ Doctors
* ★ Dentists
* ★ Pharmacists
* ★ Opticians
* ★ Attorneys
* ★ Accountants
* ★ Bankers
* ★ Insurance brokers
* ★ Investment brokers
* ★ Real estate brokers
* ★ Financial advisors
* ★ Travel agents
* ★ Collection people
* ★ Health club folks
* ★ UPS, Fed Ex, and postal workers
* ★ Anyone in sales
* ★ Professional group members

The trick to using your network to generate leads is getting organized right from the start and using the right tools. One of the best tools is the contact card.

• The Contact Card

For every contact you make you need to complete a card on that person. Otherwise, you won't know who you've called, what they said, or what your next step should be.

It's an inexpensive way to get organized, get efficient, get going, and get a job.

How to Do It

1. Get a recipe file box.

2. Get two sets of index cards with top tabs: one set numbered 1–31 for the days of the month, and one set with tabs lettered A to Z.

3. Make 200 photocopies of the contact cards in this book and cut out the cards. Or you can use 3- x 5-inch cards.

4. The cards numbered 1–31 will be used to place contacts which you are to follow up on a specific date.

5. Cards lettered A to Z are for alphabetical filing of cards you've made a contact with but have no follow up scheduled.

These names can be given to another job seeker once you've found your job. They can be given to your placement staff, if you have one. They can also be recontacted should your search exceed a reasonable time frame. If you come up with other creative ways to use them, give us a call at (800) 361-1613: we'd like to share your tricks with others.

"I've Got a Good Memory, Why Bother?" You will have to process hundreds of pieces of critical information—and you're no elephant. We can't stress strongly enough the need for detailed and accurate records.

★ This information is valuable and can't easily be replaced.

★ Most contacts require some type of follow-up.

★ You have to use some way to track your search productivity.

A Sample Contact Card

Contact _____ H/phone _____
Company _____ W/phone _____
Address _____ Fax _____
City, state, zip _____
Referred by _____ Company _____
Contact date _____
Interview information _____ Date/time _____
_____ Address _____
_____
Follow-up tasks to do:
☐ Send resume ☐ Call back ☐ Application
Follow up with _____
Notes _____
_____ (over)

- -

Contact _____ H/phone _____
Company _____ W/phone _____
Address _____ Fax _____
City, state, zip _____
Referred by _____ Company _____
Contact date _____
Interview information _____ Date/time _____
_____ Address _____
_____
Follow-up tasks to do:
☐ Send resume ☐ Call back ☐ Application
Follow up with _____
Notes _____
_____ (over)

The Unsolicited Resume Blitz

Technology has seriously changed the way people find job leads. This is especially true when it comes to getting your resume into more people's hands over long distances in less time.

• Resume-matching Services and Databases

This is an area growing by leaps and bounds. Aside from the resume-matching services provided by most of the country's job service offices, a growing number of professional/trade associations provide a resume-matching service for their memberships. The same is true of many college and university alumni associations. Make sure you look in your yellow pages to see if any new resume-matching services have sprung up in your area.

The following is a sample list of resume-matching services in operation at time of publication. For a fee these services will electronically distribute and match your information against employers' needs and distribute it to them. The way to start investigating these services is to call one, discuss cost, and get a list of employers who use that service.

We think that the money spent is worth it. It buys exposure and increases your odds of getting an unsolicited resume reviewed.

Career Database .... (508) 487-2238

Corporate Organizing and
    Research Services(CORS) .. (800) 323-1352

Datamation Databank .... (800) 860-2252

HispanData .... (805) 682-5843

Job Bank USA .... (800) 296-1872

National Employee Database .... (800) 366-3633

National Resume Bank .... (813) 896-3694

Resume-on-Computer
    (Curtis Publishing) .... (317) 636-1000

SkillSearch .... (800) 258-6641

University ProNet .... (415) 691-1600

University of California
    at Berkeley ProNet .... (800) 758-2326

Caltech ProNet .... (800) 758-1944

Carnegie Mellon ProNet .... (800) 758 2696

MIT ProNet .... (800) 758-2437

Ohio State ProNet .... (800) 758-1811

Stanford ProNet .... (800) 726-0280

UCLA ProNet .... (310) 842-0059

Michigan ProNet .... (800) 758-2644

University of Texas
    at Austin ProNet .... (800) 758-1626

The FAX.. The Whole FAX.. and nothing but the FAX.. Percentage of employers who encourage job seekers to fax their resumes: **77%** ...but only if a job opening is advertised!

• Making the Most of Resume Databases and Matching Services

Resume scanning equipment can be a good friend—or your worst enemy. The rules of resume database usage are a bit different. Computers don't think like people.

★ Send a laser-printed or typed original only—no dot matrix printing.

★ Don't use underlines, decorations, or graphics, and use 12 point type.

★ Don't fold resume—creased words don't show.

★ Don't use columns.

★ Use white paper and black print.

★ Do use technical jargon (review your career vocabulary sheet, pages 18–20).

★ Use common language—computers know synonyms.

★ Use key (job skill and transferable skills) words.

★ New graduates, use one page.

★ Make sure employment and education dates are sequential and don't conflict with each other.

★ Don't send more than one resume to a database.

★ Give specific examples of using skills you have which are directly relevant to the job.

★ Stress your most impressive qualifications.

★ Follow up in 3–4 days.

The Mass Mailing Method

We don't want to blow any smoke up your shorts here. We admit that this approach is nothing but a numbers game . . . but you don't have to do much work either.

Most job search systems have you spending bundles of time going through the library chasing down names of human resource managers, department heads, and company officers so you can direct your inquiry to them. We think this is commendable . . . but dumb!

Our advice to the serious job seeker is to purchase mailing lists. Cost? Usually around $40 for a thousand names. Consider it a tax-deductible investment. You'd spend a lot more than that in time trying to dig through the library.

One problem: Some companies that sell mailing lists have a $250 minimum. So find some other job seekers and go in together. You can select different names, save money, and break through the job search isolation. Make a friend.

We think Dun and Bradstreet provides one of the better lists. Look in your yellow pages under "Mailing Lists," call a few, and tell them the types of companies you'd like to work for, the titles of the people you want to talk with, and the zip codes of the locations you're interested in.

The Yellow Pages Index

There are about 12 million companies in the United States. Most of them are listed in the yellow pages. This gives us a clue as to one of the best ways to develop new job leads. That's right—pick up the phone! But wait—12 million companies! How do you decide which ones to call?

• Determining Your Field of Play

The process is really very easy. The first thing you need to do is to decide how far you're willing to travel to your next job.

After you've determined your acceptable commuting distance, you need to identify the communities located within that range. Assuming, for example, that you're willing to do a one-hour commute, here's what you do:

1. Get a good map of your area.

2. Get a drafting compass.

3. Find the inch-to-mile ratio on the map and set the compass to equal one hour of travel time.

4. Put the compass point on the map's location for where you live.

5. Draw a circle with the compass. Within that circle you have all of the communities located within an hour's driving time.

6. Repeat the process for ninety minutes, two hours, etc.

Now you can compile a list of those companies that fall into whichever commute range or ranges that you've chosen.

• Selecting Your Calls

The next step is to consult the yellow pages for those communities you've listed. With a highlighter in hand, turn to the index and read through the entries, asking yourself these two questions:

1. Can this type of company use my skills?

2. Would I like to use my skills in this type of company?

If you answer yes to both questions for any particular company, highlight that name. After you've finished you've got a list of prime targets for a round of phone calls. Make up a contact card (page 64) for each company, and try to call 30 companies every day.

• "But I Hate Cold Calls"

Maybe you're saying, "This sounds like a cold call to me! I hate making cold calls." Well, we didn't say this process was easy or stress-free—we just said that it works!

The Golden Rule of Cold Contacts

They work if done right—but you have to be persistent. Employers are busy people!

• Why It Works

Simple. Every employer has a phone!

Also, if you take the time to think about your geographical situation and are willing to expand your range, you can contact more companies. It's a simple equation: the more employers you contact, the better your odds of finding a job!

All About Telephone Contacts

• Call 30 Employers a Day

Once you have your contact cards, you're ready to call, generate interviews, and gather more information.

Begin with your first card and work toward your daily goal of contacting 30 bosses per day.

• Present Your Skills and Values

In Chapter 6 we discussed the skills summary card and how to turn it into a great phone script (see page 33). When you're ready to make a call, have that script with you. Make sure you have practiced it! You shouldn't have to read it— it's just there for reference. You should know it backward and forward and be so comfortable with it that you can "ad lib" as necessary.

And be ready to counter objections and accept a little rejection. Remember, you'll have more no's than yes's— about 15 no's to every yes! So don't get discouraged, keep moving forward. And document everything.

Meet Your Phone Contact Goals

Evaluate yourself. Below are 11 goals you should achieve with every phone contact.

As long as you're reaching these objectives, you're doing okay, even if an interview isn't bred from the contact.

(Look at our sample phone script on page 33 for help getting your mouth and brain to work together!)

Cold Call Strategies

To get to step 1, talking with the hiring authority, you usually have to get past a gatekeeper—the secretary or receptionist. Getting through a secretarial blockade requires learning how to respond to gatekeepers' questions. Be polite to the gatekeeper—she or he can shoot you down before you've begun to fly!

Here are a few of the blockade techniques you're likely to run up against—and some counterresponses you can use to knock them down.

1. "What is this call concerning?"

   This call is a purely personal matter. Could you put me through to him/her, please?

   or

   I was referred to Mr./Ms./Mrs._____by ____; could you put me through to him/her?

   or

   I'm trying to acquire some information that only Mr./Ms./Mrs. _____ would probably have access to.

Dialing for Dollars

Score Big with Your Telephone Contact Script

11 Steps (and 4 Goals) in Telephone Contact

1. Talk with the hiring authority
2. Identify yourself
3. Give your reason for calling (position)
4. State your experience and skills (hook)
5. Request an interview (goal #1)
   - counter objections
   - re-request interview
   - counter objections
   - re-request interview
6. Obtain an interview
7. No interview? Get referral (goal #2)
8. Collect more information (goal #3)
9. Seek future help and critique (goal #4)
10. Express thanks and close
11. Log contact

---

2. "They're busy right now. Would you care to leave a message?"

   Thanks, but I have some other business to attend to after this call. When would be a good time to call back?

3. "Is this about employment?"

   Yes, but not particularly in your company. I understand Mr./Ms./Mrs. ___ is very knowledgeable in the [occupation] field, and I was hoping he/she would volunteer a couple of minutes to help me with some career information. Could you put me through to him/her?

4. "With what company are you affiliated?"

   I don't represent a company, this is a personal research call. Could you put me through, please?

   For your last ditch effort, try this:

   I'm currently changing careers and Mr./Mrs./Ms. ___ has been recommended by [person referring you] as possibly being able to advise me. I'd appreciate talking to him/her for just a couple of minutes. Could you put me through to him/her, please?

And for your absolutely final last ditch effort:

Read your telephone contact script to the secretary (see page 33) and see if she or he knows of anyone who might be interested in someone with your qualifications, or would pass your information on.

The goal of every phone contact is to get an interview. After you've stormed the first line of defense, you'll still need to overcome a variety of obstacles in order to meet that goal.

1. "Send a resume."

Glad to. What would you like me to focus on the most? I don't want you wasting your time reading information not relevant to you.

In fact, I'm going to be in your area doing some other business. For efficiency's sake, why don't I just drop off my resume and meet you in person? When's a good time for you? Morning or afternoon— or even before or after work hours or during lunch time, if you like.

2. "We're not hiring."

I'm calling companies I think might be able to use my skills and that I'd like to work for—whether they're hiring or not. I figured I wouldn't find the hidden job market unless I looked for it, and I know that some employment situations can change rapidly. I'd like to be someone you consider should that happen.

When would be a good time for us to get together? I'd like to bring you a copy of my resume so you can have me in mind in case something develops.

3. "You need to talk to person-hell!"

Who should I talk with and may I say you sent me? Even so, I'd really appreciate a couple of minutes of your time to ask some career-related questions and shed some light on what employers are looking for from people in this line of work.

When would be a good time for us to meet—front of the week, back of the week, mornings or afternoon?

4. "We're busy, I just don't have time to talk right now."

I hope it's good busy and not stress busy! When do you foresee you may have a few spare minutes so we can get together—front of the week, back of the week, mornings or afternoons? I'm flexible.

Help Wanted!

We know that only a paltry 10 to 15 percent of the people responding to help wanted ads generate a job offer. Increase your chances of getting help wanted interviews by learning a couple of tricks and taking a little added risk.

The three most commonly asked questions about answering want ads are:

1. What's the best way to respond to a "blind ad"?

2. What's the best way to respond to requests for a salary history or salary requirements?

3. Are there any tricks for getting "in the door"?

• Blind Ads

These do not give the company name. They only give a post office box number or an employment agency. They usually represent real jobs.

Never let a blind ad put your back against the wall!

Step 1 Forget everything you think you know about answering help wanted ads.

Step 2 Get the company's name!

This is easier than you think. Find out who bought the P.O. box for the ad by calling the post office and asking the manager. If the ad was placed by a company, not an individual, they are *required* to tell you who belongs to that P.O. box. (I know what you're thinking! This can't possibly work. I learned this trick from a post office manager.) If you are unable to get this information, send in your best cover letter and resume and pray. You are now one of the hundreds of other qualified people applying for this job!

Step 3 Guess what department the advertised job title might fit under.

In our "Computer Operations" example, this job title might fit in accounting, distribution, MIS, warehousing, or maybe even just computer operations.

Step 4 Call the company, and ask for any one of these departments.

It makes no difference what department you get. It makes no difference who you get. Just reach out and touch somebody!

Step 5 Now find out where you *should be*.

When you make your first contact, with whatever department, just say, "I'm sorry that I got routed to you, I was trying to get to the people in computer operations [your desired job title]. The person on the other end will now usually tell you what department you *should* be calling.

Step 6 Call the right department and find out who's the Poobah, the big banana!

You're looking for the name of the person in charge. The hiring authority could be a department head, manager, owner, etc.

If the person you're talking with should ask: "What's this concerning?" simply say: I'm trying to send something to the head of that department and haven't got [lost, couldn't find, misplaced, never found out, etc.] their name."

Step 7 Make your phone contact, present your skills, and achieve your telephone goals (see page 67).

Now give yourself a treat. This is hard work!

• How to Respond to Questions about Salary (Be Constructive and Creative)

Salary Requirements Want ads will often request that you state your salary requirements. The general rule of thumb is not to include it—because this is a screening-out method. If you're too high, or too low, you're history. There doesn't seem to be a miracle cure for this situation, but here are some options:

★ Answer the question by stating a range.

★ Indicate your inability to address the issue until you know the details of the job and the level of responsibility it demands.

★ Indicate that income isn't your sole career concern. You have other factors to consider.

The Only Rule of Salary Disclosure

Never tell an interviewer exactly how much you made at your last job.

Salary Disclosure Want ads often ask for a salary history. This is a trap!

There's rarely a direct relationship between what you were making and what you're capable of earning. Job duties, company make-up, company size, payroll structure, and the like aren't usually the same from company to company.

• A Few Tricks

Here are a few tricks that expand your chances of getting a job offer from want ads. Although these tricks don't work every time, they work often enough to pursue.

★ Regurgitate the Ad: Make sure that your response to any ad shows how much you match up to each item listed as a qualification criterion.

★ Be Late: Answer ads about a week to ten days after they come out. This method can help keep you from the stampeding herd of resumes that will normally flood the company. (Caution: Remember this is a gimmick and you run the chance of being *too* late!)

★ Older Isn't Dead: Review older papers for want ads. It's not abnormal for an employer to *not find* the person of their employment dreams.

★ Break the Rules: Always respond by phone—even when they say not to. The risk is worth your staying apart from the flood of paper hitting an employer's desk.

★ Avoid Personnel: Try to avoid this department in the initial screening process. Always look for the hiring authority in the department with the vacancy.

★ Expand Your Job Title: Always answer the ad by saying that you'd consider other related work or, if you're calling, ask about other openings.

★ Double Your Efforts: Who says you can't respond more than one time—to the same ad! Just send the company more "pertinent" information and ask them to add into your personnel tracking folder.

★ Weasel In: Try to find a lead into the company. Do you know anyone who works at the company advertising—or someone who might know someone?

★ Expand Your Field: Don't get too wrapped up in what the employer's ad says is required for consideration. The longer the position goes unfilled, the less picky they are. If they don't find the people with those high qualifications, they rethink their criteria about 30 percent of the time.

★ No Listing Openings: Often, a listing for a job above your own skill level means someone is moving up or out of the company. This frequently opens up supporting positions that you may want to be considered for. You may want to call these folks with your telephone script.

★ Overqualification: If you're applying for a job that's below your real skill level, you may not want to include all of your academic credentials on the application form.

9 Time Management
Organizing the Campaign

A systematic approach is necessary for any successful adventure. The efforts you make to organize your campaign will reward you a hundredfold, because what you're actually doing is creating a support system for yourself.

Your support system should include:

★ Tools—to make your job easier

★ A process—to follow on a daily basis

★ Helping agencies—to support your efforts (see Appendix D—Resources)

Tools of the Trade

Job finding is a required madness— for those who aren't organized! But if you have the right tools to help you organize your time and activity, you can decrease the stress substantially. Do you have the tools you need to succeed?

• Basic Job Search Tools

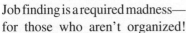

Certain basic tools are necessary for an efficient and successful job search. These include a work space; office supplies; job lead resources, organizers, and tracking materials; and access to a word processor and computer. Two other very important tools are your Weekly Planner and your Activity Tracking Chart. (These are so critical to your job search efforts that we will discuss them in detail in a page or two.)

1. Work space: An area where you and your tools will not be disturbed, with access to a phone

2. Writing, note-taking, and mailing supplies

3. Other office supplies

4. Job lead development and tracking materials
   • Subscriptions to all the newspapers in your geographical job search area, plus the *National Business Employment Weekly,* if you're targeting the whole country

   • Yellow pages from all the towns and cities in your geographical job search area

   • Weekly planner and activity tracking chart (see pages 72–73)

   • File folders (50 to start) and a file carton to hold them. You'll need to keep records on various companies

5. Access to word processing

If you don't have your own computer, find a friend or hire someone to word process your resume, cover letter, and skills summary card. Using a computer to create these documents will make it easier to make changes if you need to later on.

• The Weekly Planner

One of the most successful—if not simply the best—tools for organizing is the weekly planner. This simple and handy device will help you to structure your time and to keep track of your appointments—a number one priority.

You can buy a weekly planner at any stationery or office supply store, or you can photocopy the forms we're providing here. We suggest you make 20 copies. But if you're being as active in your job search as you should be, you probably won't need them all—you'll end up with a new job before you run out!

A couple of tips:

1. Track *only* your job-related appointments.

2. Don't overschedule your time—anytime!

For more comprehensive information about organization and forms, we recommend *The Job Search Time Manager* by William S. Frank (Berkeley, CA: Ten Speed Press, 1993).

The Daily Action Plan

Process is often as important as substance in a job search. In other words, *how* you do your job search tasks can be as important as the tasks themselves. What's the good of getting everything done if you're a stressed-out basket case at the end of the day?

Weekly Planner

Interviews & Appointments

Monday's Date: _____

Morning _____

7:00 _____

8:00 _____

9:00 _____

10:00 _____

11:00 _____

Noon _____

1:00 _____

2:00 _____

3:00 _____

4:00 _____

5:00 _____

Evening _____

Interviews & Appointments

Tuesday's Date: _____

Morning _____

7:00 _____

8:00 _____

9:00 _____

10:00 _____

11:00 _____

Noon _____

1:00 _____

2:00 _____

3:00 _____

4:00 _____

5:00 _____

Evening _____

Interviews & Appointments

Wednesday's Date: _____

Morning _____

7:00 _____

8:00 _____

9:00 _____

10:00 _____

11:00 _____

Noon _____

1:00 _____

2:00 _____

3:00 _____

4:00 _____

5:00 _____

Evening _____

Interviews & Appointments

Thursday's Date: _____

Morning _____

7:00 _____

8:00 _____

9:00 _____

10:00 _____

11:00 _____

Noon _____

1:00 _____

2:00 _____

3:00 _____

4:00 _____

5:00 _____

Evening _____

Interviews & Appointments

Friday's Date: _____

Morning _____

7:00 _____

8:00 _____

9:00 _____

10:00 _____

11:00 _____

Noon _____

1:00 _____

2:00 _____

3:00 _____

4:00 _____

5:00 _____

Evening _____

Measure Your Weekly Activity

Number

Phone contacts _____

Resumes sent _____

Applications _____

Interviews _____

How well are you hanging in?

The Golden Rule of Job Search Action

Try to schedule your interviews
in the afternoon and do all your calling
in the morning!

Activity Tracking Chart / Month: _____

Date	Employer phone contacts	Resumes and cover letters sent	Personal network contacts	Applications returned to employers	Companies researched	Hours spent in search activity
1	_____	_____	_____	_____	_____	_____
2	_____	_____	_____	_____	_____	_____
3	_____	_____	_____	_____	_____	_____
4	_____	_____	_____	_____	_____	_____
5	_____	_____	_____	_____	_____	_____
6	_____	_____	_____	_____	_____	_____
7	_____	_____	_____	_____	_____	_____
8	_____	_____	_____	_____	_____	_____
9	_____	_____	_____	_____	_____	_____
10	_____	_____	_____	_____	_____	_____
11	_____	_____	_____	_____	_____	_____
12	_____	_____	_____	_____	_____	_____
13	_____	_____	_____	_____	_____	_____
14	_____	_____	_____	_____	_____	_____
15	_____	_____	_____	_____	_____	_____
16	_____	_____	_____	_____	_____	_____
17	_____	_____	_____	_____	_____	_____
18	_____	_____	_____	_____	_____	_____
19	_____	_____	_____	_____	_____	_____
20	_____	_____	_____	_____	_____	_____
21	_____	_____	_____	_____	_____	_____
22	_____	_____	_____	_____	_____	_____
23	_____	_____	_____	_____	_____	_____
24	_____	_____	_____	_____	_____	_____
25	_____	_____	_____	_____	_____	_____
26	_____	_____	_____	_____	_____	_____
27	_____	_____	_____	_____	_____	_____
28	_____	_____	_____	_____	_____	_____
29	_____	_____	_____	_____	_____	_____
30	_____	_____	_____	_____	_____	_____
31	_____	_____	_____	_____	_____	_____

Establishing a daily activity sequence—a daily action plan—will help you get your tasks done efficiently, minimize stress, and keep you humming along in the job search groove.

The following plan is the one we advise for you—at least until you develop your own rhythm and create a process that's comfortable for you and accommodates your needs and lifestyle.

1. Wake early and get all the family, personal, and extraneous stuff out of the way (breakfast, clean-up, kiss the spouse, pet the dog/cat/goldfish, tell the kids you love 'em, etc.).

2. Review your weekly planner and your job lead organizer (see pages 72–73) for today's date and follow up as needed.

   • If you have an upcoming interview, call and gather information about that company.

   • Send cover letters and resumes to the previous day's contacts.

   • Return any calls you are supposed to.

   • Contact all the people you couldn't get through to yesterday.

   • Send a thank-you note to anyone you interviewed with yesterday or anyone who has been of significant help.

3. Make sure you have 30 *new* prospect cards to contact on this day. These can come from the yellow pages (see page 66) or from any other source you've developed.

4. Read the want ads—don't even look at the rest of the paper until this part's done.

   • Respond by phone, if possible.

   • Respond with paper, if necessary.

5. Make contact with your 30 *new* prospects.

• The Activity Tracking Chart

Tracking progress is crucial to reaching any goal. With our activity tracking chart, you can see if you're really meeting your daily objectives. If not, adjust your approach and reorganize your time as needed.

Directions: Make copies of this form—one per month. Review your job search day and enter the correct numbers under each title.

10 The Job Offer

Accepting a Job Offer Is More Than Just Saying Yes!

Determining if a job offer is good for you isn't as simple as it seems. Ask yourself what the perfect job looks like. Your mind will immediately paint you a glowing, rosy picture. But can you identify the factors that go into the picture? That's exactly what you need to do when you get an actual job offer.

Here's a way to evaluate every offer you receive according to eleven major categories. Make a copy of this for each job, and fill in the pertinent information. This will put all the issues out in front of you in an organized way so that you can get a clear picture of the job you're considering—*before* you make that important decision.

• Job Factors to Consider Before Saying Yes

Why are you considering the job?

★ Pure survival
★ A positive career move

Financial

★ Gross income
★ Commissions
★ Bonuses
★ Car(s)
★ Expense account
★ Retirement plan
★ Stock options, investment plans
★ Profit sharing
★ Severance package
★ Relocation assistance
★ Cost-of-living increases

Career Advancement

★ Pay raise criteria and schedule
★ Frequency of appraisals (the more often the better!)
★ Advancement opportunity
★ Advancement criteria

Insurance

★ Medical
★ Life
★ Disability
★ Dental
★ Optical
★ Mental health

Environment

★ Will you like the coworkers?
★ Will you like the supervisor's style?

Job Security

★ Is the career field growing?
★ Are the number of employees growing?
★ Has the company recently laid off?
★ Will you need to learn new skills to keep your job?
★ Will NAFTA, GATT, or other government deals affect you?

Stress

★ Frequency of overtime
★ Frequency of weekend or holiday work
★ Travel demands
★ Deadline, quota, or quality demands
★ Environmental hazards (noise, chemicals, heat/cold, etc.)

Job Duties and Responsibilities

★ Will you enjoy your daily job functions?
★ Will your level of authority be satisfying for you?
★ Will you be comfortable reporting to the person who is your supervisor?

★ How will you be evaluated?

★ What are the supervisor's biggest problems?

Educational

★ Personal tuition reimbursement

★ Family tuition reimbursement

★ Professional association memberships

★ Willingness to send you to seminars

Vacation and Sick Leave

★ How do you accrue vacation time?

★ Allowable days per year

★ When you can take them

★ Days of sick leave before disciplinary action?

Other Benefits

★ Child care

★ Club memberships

★ Outplacement assistance

★ Company loans/credit unions

★ Time off for military commitments

• A Final Word

As you can see from our chart, using creativity, personal contacts, and networks accounts for most of the employment in the country. This is the assertive and creative method we've been outlining for you as you work through these 88 pages to your next job.

Comparative Success of Different Job Search Methods

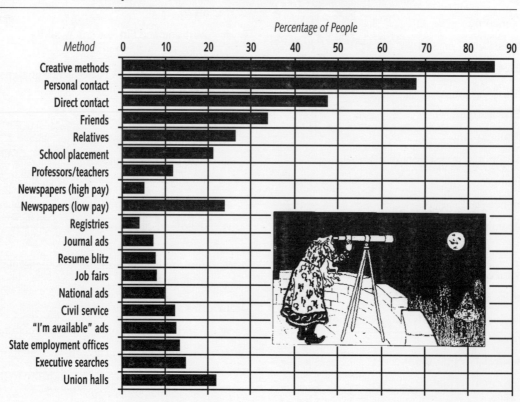

Percentage of People

Method

	0	10	20	30	40	50	60	70	80	90
Creative methods										
Personal contact										
Direct contact										
Friends										
Relatives										
School placement										
Professors/teachers										
Newspapers (high pay)										
Newspapers (low pay)										
Registries										
Journal ads										
Resume blitz										
Job fairs										
National ads										
Civil service										
"I'm available" ads										
State employment offices										
Executive searches										
Union halls										

Appendix A

Job Titles

Abstractor
Accountant
Accountant, Chief
Accounting Analyst
Accounting Assistant
Accounting Clerk
Accounting Manager
Accounting Supervisor
Accounting Technician
Accounts Payable Assistant
Accounts Payable Processing Clerk
Accounts Payable/Receivable Manager
Accounts Receivable Assistant
Accounts Receivable Clerk
Activity Coordinator
Administrative Assistant
Administrative Clerk
Administrative Secretary
Administrative Support Supervisor
Admissions Counselor
Admitting Representative
Adolescent Program Coordinator
Advertising and Sales Coordinator
Aeronautical Engineer
Affirmative Action Officer
Aircraft Maintenance Superintendent
Aircraft Maintenance Technician
Analyst/Programmer
Analyst/Programmer, Financial
Applications Engineer
Applications Programmer
Assembly Supervisor
Asset Adjuster
Audiologist
Audiovisual Specialist

Audit and Control Specialist
Auditor
Auditor, Internal

Benefit Manager
Benefit Specialist
Billing Supervisor
Biomedical Engineer Technician
Bookkeeper
Box Plant Manager
Branch Manager
Budget Analyst
Budget and Finance Manager
Budget Assistant
Budget Associate
Building Inspector
Building Inspector Trainee
Buyer

Carpenter
Chart Analyst/Clerk
Chauffeur
Chemical Coatings Manager
Chemical Engineer
Cleaning Assistant
Cleaning Supervisor
Clerk Typist
Clinical Program Supervisor
Clinical Supervisor
Clinical Technician
Coder and Abstractor
Collateral Asset Adjuster
Collection and Exchange Teller
Collections Analyst
Collections Clerk
Collections Supervisor

Collector
Communications Specialist
Community Relations Specialist
Compensation Manager
Computer Operations Specialist
Computer Operations Supervisor
Computer Operator
Computer Programmer
Confidential Secretary
Configuration Engineer
Consultant
Consultant Trainer
Controller
Cook
Corporate Communications Manager
Cost Accountant
Cost Analysis Estimator
Cost Analyst
Cost Estimate Analyst
Counselor, Guidance
Credit Analyst
Credit Clerk
Credit Manager
Criminal Investigator
Custodial Service Manager
Custodian
Customer Engineer
Customer Satisfaction Analyst
Customer Service Clerk
Customer Service Manager
Customer Service Representative
Customer Service Specialist

Data Entry Operator
Data Entry Supervisor
Data Management Specialist

Data Processing Control Assistant

Data Processing Hardware Specialist

Data Processing Manager

Data Processing Operations Supervisor

Data Processing Operator

Data Processing Production Coordinator

Database Administrative Manager

Database Analyst

Decision Support Consultant

Design Engineer

Development Officer, Economic

Dietary Department Aide

Dietitian

District Sales Manager

Document Control Clerk

Document Reproduction and
Control Specialist

Document Reproduction and
Control Supervisor

Draft/Design Checker

Drafter

Driver

Economic Development Officer

Editor

Educator

EEG Technician

EEO Manager

EKG Technician

Electrician

Electronics Assembler

Electronics Assembly Supervisor

Electronics Engineer

Electronics Technician

Employee Benefits Administrator

Employee Relations Coordinator

Engineer

Engineering Administrator

Engineering and Plant
Maintenance Superintendent

Engineering Manager

Engineering Manager, Manufacturing

Engineering Technician

Equipment and Facilities Manager

Equipment Operator

Estimator, Cost Analyst

Evaluation Specialist, Vocational

Executive Secretary

Expeditor

Facilities and Equipment Manager

Facilities Coordinator

Facilities Planning and
Special Projects Coordinator

Factory Clerk

Field Engineer

Field Service Engineer Technician

File Clerk

Financial and Budget Assistant

Financial Aid Counselor

Financial Aid Officer

Financial Analyst

Financial Analyst, Senior

Financial Applications
Programmer/Analyst

Financial Manager

Financial Supervisor

Fire Fighter

First-Aid Attendant

Food Service Worker

Foreperson

Foreperson/Inspector

Forklift Mechanic

Forklift Operator

Grants Coordinator

Graphic Artist

Graphics Manager

Greaser/Oiler

Grounds Maintenance Supervisor

Groundskeeper

Hand Packer

Handler, Material

Hazardous Materials Investigation
Specialist

Health Educator, Staff Development

Heavy Equipment Operator

Histologic Technician

Housekeeper

Housekeeping Porter

Human Resources Administrator

Human Resources Assistant

Human Resources Development
Supervisor

Human Resources Manager

Human Resources Representative

Hygienist, Industrial

Illustrator, Graphic

Industrial Engineer

Industrial Nurse

Industrial/Material Handling Engineer

Information Specialist

Information Systems Senior
Vice President

Inspector

Inspector and Testing General
Supervisor

Inspector, Chief

Instructor, Skills

Instrumentation Engineer

Insurance Department Supervisor

Interviewer, Loan

Inventory Control Manager

Inventory Supervisor

Investigator

Job Analyst

Labor Relations Analyst

Laboratory Aide

Laborer

Landscape Specialist

Laundry Manager

Laundry Worker

Leasing Agent

Legal Compliance Specialist

Librarian

Library Assistant

Lift Truck Operator

Loan Adjuster

Loan Interviewer

Loan Officer

Machine Clerk

Machine Operator/Case Maker

Machine Operator, Packing

Machinist

Mailroom Clerk

Maintenance Electrician

Maintenance Engineer

Maintenance Manager

Maintenance Mechanic

Maintenance Supervisor

Maintenance Technician

Maintenance Worker

Maintenance Worker, Assistant

Management Information Systems
    Manager

Management Trainee

Manager of Consumer Affairs

Manager of Database Administration

Manufacturing Engineer

Manufacturing Engineering Manager

Manufacturing Quality Engineering
    Manager

Market Research Manager

Marketing Associate

Marketing Coordinator

Marketing Manager

Marketing Trainee

Material Expediter

Material Handling Supervisor

Material Supervisor

Materials Handler

Materials Manager

Mechanic

Mechanical Engineer

Mechanic's Helper

Medical Technologist

Medical Transcriber

Merchandise Coordinator

Merchandising Assistant

Messenger

Microbiologist

Microfilm Clerk

Millwright

Mortgage Processing Clerk

New Accounts Clerk

Note Teller

Nurse, Charge

Nurse, Industrial

Nurse, Licensed Practical (LPN)

Nurse, Licensed Vocational (LVN)

Nurse, Occupational Health

Nurse, Public Health

Nurse, Registered (RN)

Nurse, School

Nurse's Aide

Nutrition Educator

Occupational Therapist

Office Administrator

Office Assistant

Office Manager

Office Supervisor

Office Systems Coordinator

Operations Analyst

Operations Manager

Operations Officer

Operations Support Specialist

Outpatient Program Coordinator

Outside Sales Representative

Packer

Packing Machine Operator

Painter

Payroll Accountant

Payroll Clerk

Payroll Manager

PBX Operator/Receptionist

Personal Assistant

Pharmacist

Pharmacy Assistant

Pharmacy Technician Supervisor

Phlebotomist

Phototype Assembler

Physical Therapist

Physical Therapy Assistant

Physician

Pilot

Pipe Fitter

Planner

Plant Coordinator

Plant Maintenance Engineer

Plant Manager

Police Officer

Police Records Clerk

Porter

Printing Press Operator

Product Consultant

Product Development Technician

Production Clerk

Production Control Clerk

Production Control Manager

Production Coordinator

Production Foreman/Supervisor

Production Planner

Production Scheduler

Production Supervisor

Program Manager

Programmer

Programmer, Senior Applications

Programmer, Systems

Programmer/Analyst

Programmer/Analyst, Financial
    Applications

Project Analyst

Project Director

Project Engineer

Project Leader

Project Manager

Project Quality Engineer

Proof Machine Operator

Public Information Representative

Public Safety Administrative Assistant

Publications Artist

Purchasing Agent

Purchasing Assistant/Associate

Purchasing Manager

Quality Assurance Coordinator

Quality Assurance Manager

Quality Assurance/Utilization Review
   Analyst

Quality Control Manager

Quality Engineer

Quality Specialist/Auditor

Radio Dispatcher

Radiology Technologist

Receiving Inspector

Receptionist

Receptionist/Secretary

Regional Retail Sales Manager

Registered Staff Pharmacist

Repairperson

Research Engineer

Respiratory Therapist

Retail Products-Direct Sales Manager

Retail Sales Manager

Risk Manager

Safety and Physical Security
   Coordinator

Safety Engineer

Safety Manager

Safety Officer

Sales Administrator

Sales and Advertising Coordinator

Sales Assistant

Sales Manager

Sales Promoter

Sales Representative

Scientific Programmer

Secretary

Secretary/Receptionist

Security Guard

Security Manager

Security Supervisor

Service Worker, Vehicle

Sheet Metal Worker

Shipping and Receiving Clerk

Shipping and Receiving Supervisor

Shop Supervisor

Site Messenger

Software Configuration Specialist

Special Accounts Manager

Speech Pathologist

Staffing Coordinator

State Police Officer

Statistical Analyst

Statistician

Stock Clerk

Stock Supervisor

Storeroom Attendant

Survey Party Chief

Surveyor

System Security Specialist

Systems Analyst

Systems and Programming Manager

Systems Coordinator

Systems Programmer

Systems Software Engineer

Tape Librarian

Teacher, College

Teacher, Elementary School

Teacher, Kindergarten

Teacher, Secondary School

Teacher's Aide

Technical Analyst

Technical Services Representative

Technical Writer

Technician

Telemarketing Manager

Telemarketing Representative

Telemarketing Sales Manager

Telemarketing Sales Representative

Teller

Test Engineer

Test Engineering Manager

Test Technician

Tool and Die Maker

Traffic Clerk

Traffic Manager

Training and Development Director

Training Associate

Training Consultant

Training Manager

Training Representative

Travel Agent

Travel Coordinator

Treasurer, Corporate

Truck Mechanic

Trust Officer

Video Specialist

Vocational Evaluation Specialist

Wage and Salary Administrator

Wang System Administrator

Ward Clerk

Warehouse Manager

Welder

Word Processor

Workers' Compensation Manager

Appendix B

Disability Issues

Yes, some employers still do discriminate. However, with the passage of the Americans with Disabilities Act (ADA) in 1992, employers must now follow certain regulations. For more information on the ADA, or a copy of the law, call or write the EEOC Office of Communications and Legislative Affairs, 1801 L Street, N.W., Washington, D.C. 20507; (800) 669-EEOC.

• What are the rules?

There is only one rule you need to know—the **Essential Functions Rule**. And it goes like this: If you can perform the "essential functions" (the fundamentals, the critical duties) of the job, the employer can't discriminate against you in the hiring process.

• What They Can Ask

Interviewers can ask you any questions directly related to the "essential functions" of the job for which you are applying.

- ★ Can you lift a 50-pound box?
- ★ Can you stand (or sit) for extended periods?
- ★ Can you be at work by 9 A.M. every day?
- ★ Can you work five days a week?
- ★ Can you reach the top of a six-foot-high filing cabinet?
- ★ Do you have a driver's license?
- ★ What were your duties on your previous job, and what accommodations were made to facilitate your work?
- ★ Can you perform the job for which you are applying with or without accommodation?

They can also ask you to demonstrate how you would perform a particular job task.

• What They Can't Ask

- ★ Have you ever been treated for the following conditions or diseases?

- ★ Has anyone in your family ever had any of the following listed illnesses?
- ★ Have you ever been hospitalized? For what?
- ★ List any conditions or illnesses for which you've been treated in the past three years.
- ★ Have you ever been treated for a mental disorder?
- ★ Are you taking any medication?
- ★ Have you ever been treated for drug addiction or alcoholism?
- ★ Do you have any major physical disabilities? If so, how did your disability come about? What is the prognosis for recovery?
- ★ Have you ever filed for worker's compensation benefits?
- ★ How many times were you absent from your previous job because of illness?
- ★ Do you have any disabilities that would affect your performance in the position for which you are applying?

• What to Do If the Interviewer Asks You an Illegal Question!

Give the poor interviewer, who may not be familiar with the ADA rules, a break before jumping down his or her throat. Just ask: *Can you tell me how this question relates to the job so I can give you my best answer?* This gives the interviewer a warning that they're treading on thin legal ice—but nicely.

• What about Physical Examinations?

Drug tests and physicals are pretty much a fact of life—even with the ADA regulations going your way. The rule is this: Physicals should be performed only after a conditional job offer.

• Does the Employer's Insurance Rate Go Up When a Disabled Person Is Hired?

There are a number of variables that can affect whether or not it does—including size of the company, work environment and type of work, the presence of unions at the company, whether the employer is private or a government agency, and where the company is located. In general, however, the answer is no, the presence of a disabled worker will not drive up the insurance rate—or will increase it by so little that the cost is easily offset by a good worker's productivity and loyalty.

The employer's idea that the insurance will go up can still be a big problem for a disabled applicant though—so come to the interview with ammunition! Call a few local insurance companies before the interview; describe the job, the company, and your disability, and ask how the employer's insurance might change. Chances are good that most of them will tell you it won't go up, or not by much—share this information with the interviewer if the issue arises. You should be able to reassure the employer—and also show by your research that you have their best interests in mind!

Disability Facts

Number of Disabled Americans Working = Over 14 million

This figure includes over 63,000 people diagnosed HIV positive or with AIDS and 2 million diabetics. Of all the people diagnosed with multiple sclerosis, 86 percent are working, while 78 percent of white-collar workers with cancer are on the job and 63 percent of blue-collar cancer victims are on the job.

• Disclosure Conflict: If, When, and How to Tell

No easy decisions here! You have a number of disclosure options, some better than others—and you have a few issues to consider.

Issue 1: To Disclose or Not? If you have an invisible disability, such as a mental illness or heart trouble, and it won't affect your ability to perform the job, there may be no need to disclose the issue at all. A visible disability will obviously disclose itself in the interview if you have not already told the employer about it.

Issue 2: Employers Don't Like Surprises In fact, we've found that most employers would rather know about a person's disability before they actually meet you. This brings us to the next issue.

Issue 3: When and How to Disclose Your Disability Experience has shown that the best way to disclose your disability is with the help of a third party. This could be the person referring you for the position, a former employer, or the people you chose as references.

These folks can prepare the interviewer, dispelling any incorrect preconceptions an employer might have about your abilities. If you're not fortunate enough to have this kind of support, your next best option is to call them and let them know before the interview—especially if your disability is a visible one—or let them know when you accept the job offer if your disability is not visible but you choose to disclose it at this point.

The easiest ways to hang yourself:

★ Let them know in your cover letter/resume.

★ Include the information in your skills summary card.

★ Let people know as you develop job leads.

★ Tell the telephone screening interviewer.

★ Put the information on your application.

The Best Way Is to Ask for Help

For more help with issues of disclosure and your rights, call:

The Disability Rights Education and Defense Fund (800) 466-4232 (also provides referrals, assistance, and ADA text)

The Mental Health Law Project (202) 467-5730

or your local United Way Agency

• Dispel the Interviewer's Fears

Employers are afraid they'll make a mistake with the new regulations. It may be up to you to make the interviewer feel at ease and address their concerns about hiring a person with a disability.

A sample script

I realize that employers have a tougher job of selecting applicants now with all of the governmental regulations like the ADA. I'm probably as nervous about talking about my capabilities as you are about asking questions about them. So, if you don't mind, I'd like to put both of us more at ease by addressing some of the concerns I think employers have—and please don't hesitate asking about my abilities to perform the basic functions of the job for which I'm applying.

At this point you can address the following issues: terminations, attendance, job site modification, safety, training, and getting along with other people.

Termination Dispel the myth that getting rid of you for poor work performance is any more difficult than for any other person.

Attendance This is one of the employer's biggest concerns. You have to tell the employer how you'll get to work and convince the employer that you'll have as good, or better, attendance than other workers.

Job Site Modification Know what's needed to modify your work site and don't be overly demanding.

Safety You have to convey that you'll be able to deal with emergency situations. Tell the interviewer how you'd handle a fire or other physically demanding situations.

Training Employers may be erroneously concerned about a disabled person's ability to learn complex tasks and gain new knowledge. Give them examples of when you've developed new skills.

Getting Along This is a biggie! Stress instances when you've developed positive relationships with coworkers or fellow students.

The Diabilities Rule of Leverage: Positives Can Counterbalance Negatives

Appendix C

Drug Testing

Over half of America's employers are testing people for drug use, both before they hire them and randomly throughout their tenure with the company. Whether you think drug testing is an intrusion on your personal life or not, it is the price you'll pay to enter many companies.

• "It's None of Their Business! (Is It?)"

**Drug Use Becomes a Problem
the Minute Anyone's Life is
Negatively Affected by Your Behavior!**

Why is it any of the employer's business what you do on your own time? Simple! *Small Business Reports* estimated that it cost employers over $60 billion in lost productivity in 1993 alone to carry the monkey on your back.

Data supports what employers already know. Drugged and drunk workers are:

★ Three times more likely to be late or absent

★ Three times more likely to use health benefits

★ Four times more likely to file for worker's compensation

Of the 10 million work-related accidents per year:

★ 47 percent are alcohol-related

★ 2 million result in claims against employers

• What Drugs Do They Test For?
(And How Do They Test for Them?)

Drug screening is done by use of urine or saliva samples. Only a few drops are needed to detect the following types of substances.

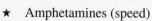

★ Amphetamines (speed)

★ Barbiturates (downers)

★ Benzodiazepines (tranquilizers)

★ Opiates

★ Cocaine

★ Painkillers

★ Marijuana

★ Methaqualone (Quaaludes)

★ Alcohol

★ PCP

• How Long Do Drugs Stay in the Body?

Everybody's different. Factors affecting the results can include: weight, physical activity, diet, frequency of drug use, longevity of use, drug potency, etc. The table below gives some statistics on drug retention. But we think you'd be a fool to bet your job and career on these figures.

Drug Retention*	
Drug	*Duration in Body*
Amphetamines	1–2 days
Barbiturates	1–3 days (short-acting)
	1–3 weeks (long-acting)
Benzodiazepines	1–14 days
Opiates	1–3 days
Cocaine	2–3 days
Pain killers	2–3 days
Marijuana	1–7 days (1–2 joints/week)
	1–4 weeks (3+ joints/week)

*"Drug Testing in the Workplace," Holly Atkinson, *New Woman Magazine*, 1988.

• Can Someone Beat the Test?

Yes, we know of a few people who've used herbs to flush out their system and gotten away with it. But—they ended up losing their jobs for poor performance.

If you're stupid enough to get loaded before the drug test, you just might be too dumb to work!

• Do Many People Fail Their Drug Test?

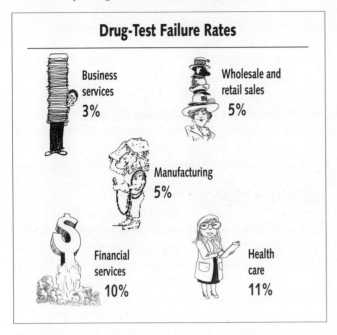

Drug-Test Failure Rates

Business services
3%

Wholesale and retail sales
5%

Manufacturing
5%

Financial services
10%

Health care
11%

Sort of makes you wonder about the people handling our money and our health care—now doesn't it?

• Can the Test Results Be Wrong?

Yes, but don't count on anyone admitting it!

Some studies say that up to 5 percent of test results are inaccurate due to human error, tricks used by the testee, and the normal margin of error in any chemical testing. Five percent doesn't sound like much until you realize that this translates into about 2 million people who might not get or keep a job because of a "false positive."

• What Might Cause a "False Positive"?

The most common causes of false positives are over-the-counter drugs and the things you eat or drink. The following common items can show up as one of the drugs for which you're being tested:

★ Appetite suppressants

★ Decongestants

★ Sleeping pills

★ Antidiarrhea drugs

★ Some herbal teas

★ Antipsychotic drugs

★ Pain killers

★ Asthma medication

★ Anticonvulsants

★ Circulation medication

★ Cough syrups

★ Poppy seeds (yes, it's true)

★ Antidepressants

★ Cold syrups

• How to Get a Fair Shake

In reality, you have very little recourse against a false positive. You can fight it, but can you afford the fight?

Your best plan is to plan ahead. Know what your test results will be before you take one. Have an independent test (a blood test requesting specific drug screening) done a couple of days before your test.

If you're unable to do this, your next best way to insure against a false positive is to ask for a blood test instead of a urine test—even if you have to pay for it yourself. Blood tests are more specific.

And finally, make a list of all the foods you've eaten and medications taken, give it to the tester, and ask if any of these might show up as a positive on the drug screen.

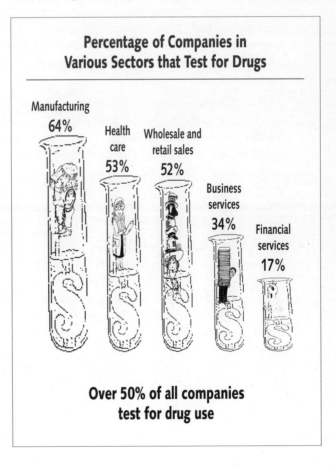

Percentage of Companies in Various Sectors that Test for Drugs

Manufacturing
64%

Health care
53%

Wholesale and retail sales
52%

Business services
34%

Financial services
17%

Over 50% of all companies test for drug use

Appendix D

Resources

Helping Agencies

When all else fails, yell for help. But yell for the right kind—from the right people!

Let's Swap: A Free Gift if you participate in a research project!

We want information on how people find jobs—unusual search methods, job search stories, etc. If we can use it in our next book, we'll send you a free Wizard of Work gift. Write: Job Search Training Systems, 7648 Indian Cherry Drive, Nineveh, IN 46164. Call: (800) 361-1613.

Or, send us copies of your Activity Tracking Chart. We'll send you a free Wizard of Work gift for that, too.Government Systems

★ **ETA** There is one system that can be of immense help—if you're willing to jump through the hoops. The U.S. Department of Labor's Employment and Training Administration (ETA). There is an ETA job service office in virtually every community.

★ **JTPA Offices** A range of employment offices or agencies are supported by the Job Training Partnership Act. There are about 600 of them across the country, and they've had a fair share of success working with welfare recipients, dislocated workers, and youth. Contact the Department of Labor at (202) 219-6666 for the office or agency in your area.

★ **Elected Officials** These folks work for you, even when you're not working yourself. Don't hesitate to call them and tell them what you've done and ask for help—and keep asking for help—and keep asking for help. Remember the cardinal rule of politics: "The squeaky wheel gets the grease."

A note to veterans: There's a new law (the Service Members Occupational Training Act, or SMOCTA) in place to help newer veterans reenter the labor force. Go to your ETA job service office and request your well-earned preferential treatment. In some instances, employers are given compensation for hiring veterans.

Job Search Clubs

A job search club is a structured group of people who are serious about looking for work—it's not a place to sleep or blow off time. The club usually has a group leader. Everyone shares his or her information and experiences, and helps one another develop leads.

You can either join a preexisting job club or set up one of your own. Get everyone you know who's unemployed and ask your local ETA job service office or JTPA agency to help you set up a club. If you're a student, ask your placement staff to help you set one up. If you're over forty we strongly advise that you find or form a "40+ club" in your area.

If you need help finding or setting up a job search club, contact the National Association of Job Search Trainers at (606) 257-6576.

**To be unemployed and independent...
is almost an impossibility!**

More Help for the Job-Hunter

BLUE COLLAR AND BEYOND
Sample Resumes for Skilled Trades and Services
by Yana Parker

What we once called "blue collar" jobs have expanded to include all kinds of work—not just auto repair and construction, but food service, hospitality, clerical support, health and beauty, and so on. These jobs often require resumes, but most resume books don't address them. Here, in her trademark straightforward, action-oriented style, resume expert Yana Parker gives the basics of resume writing—including dealing with difficult or embarrassing issues—and provides well over 100 sample resumes to show how it's done.
192 pages

DYNAMIC COVER LETTERS
by Katharine Hansen & Randall Hansen

This book shows how to sell yourself to absolutely any employer, with a tailor-made letter that will get your resume read, get you an interview . . . and land you that job. Chock-full of sample letters that show the right and wrong ways to answer an ad, ask for an interview, explain gaps in your resume, and much, much more. Includes brand-new information on job-hunting using the Internet.
160 pages

WHAT COLOR IS YOUR PARACHUTE?
A Practical Manual for Job Hunters & Career Changers
by Richard Nelson Bolles

The classic in the field for over 25 years, PARACHUTE is updated every year, with solid advice on every aspect of job-hunting, from figuring out what you really want to do to landing the job of your dreams. Millions of readers have used the sensible advice, helpful exercises, and bountiful resources to find career happiness.
480 pages

And now, PARACHUTE is also available on cassette! Read by Richard Bolles himself, this 8-tape set covers everything the job-seeker needs, in convenient audio format. Also includes the New Quick Job-Hunting Map, a handy 48-page workbook.

COLLEGE DEGREES BY MAIL
by John Bear, Ph.D.

It is genuinely possible to earn a legitimate, career-oriented, fully accredited college degree (Bachelor's, Master's, Doctorate, even Law) without spending one semester on campus. This book shows how—by mail, over computer lines, through exams, and by other methods. Gives full information on the top 100 nonresident schools.
216 pages

For more information, or to order, call the publisher at the number below. We accept VISA, Mastercard, and American Express. You may also wish to write for our free catalog of over 500 books, posters, and audiotapes.

Ten Speed Press   P.O. Box 7123   Berkeley, CA 94707
800-841-BOOK